Grace People

'This book relates detailed biblical interpretation to life right now and invites our response to the God of the Bible, 'for it is the God who said, "let light shine out of darkness", who has shone in our hearts to give the light of the knowledge of the glory of God in the face of Jesus Christ' (2 Cor. 4:6). This book is written for believers. I pray that the time they spend with *Grace People* in one hand and the Bible in the other will deepen their relationship with Christ and fire them up to witness for Him. I commend this book most warmly.'

The Most Revd and Rt Hon Dr John Sentamu, Archbishop of York

'By emphasizing the secure biblical foundations of God's covenant love for His people, Michael Baughen characteristically helps us to understand God's promises in the context of our daily lives, and encourages us in practical ways to do all that we can develop a closer relationship with him. A great devotional help.'

The Rt Revd Prebendary Sandy Millar, St Mark Tollington Park

'This is an accessible and comprehensive survey of a key theme in Scripture by an outstanding biblical expositor. I found it both encouraging and challenging as it opened my eyes to the depth of God's grace and the practical implications of our covenant discipleship. It relates to some major contemporary issues (such as the environment) and is firmly rooted in personal experience. An illuminating and inspiring book which warms the heart as well as stimulating the mind.'

Rt Revd James Newcome, Bishop of Penrith

'This is a book to instruct the mind but also to warm the heart. It takes us through the sweep of the bible teaching on God's covenant of Grace, all brought to life through Michael's humanity and sheer enthusiasm. Read and be drawn again to that amazing grace!'

Steve James, Rector designate, Holy Trinity Platt, Manchester

'Michael Baughen writes with infectious enthusiasm about the vital subject of God's covenants. An unusual and valuable feature are the Pauses for Reflection and Response.'

Revd Canon Andrew Cormes, All Saints, Crowborough

Grace People

ROOTED IN GOD'S COVENANT LOVE

Michael Baughen

Copyright © 2006 Michael Baughen

12 11 10 09 08 07 06   7 6 5 4 3 2 1

First published in 2006 by Keswick Ministries and Authentic Media
9 Holdom Avenue, Bletchley, Milton Keynes, Bucks., MK1 1QR, UK
and PO Box 1047, Waynesboro, GA 30830-2047, USA
www.authenticmedia.co.uk
Authentic Media is a division of Send the Light Ltd.,
a company limited by guarantee (registered charity no 270162)

The right of Michael Baughen to be
identified as the author of this work has been
asserted by him in accordance with the
Copyright, Designs and Patents Act 1988.

British Library Cataloguing in Publication Data

A catalogue record for this book is available from the British Library

ISBN-13: 978-85078-695-5
ISBN-10: 1-85078-695-X

Unless otherwise stated, Scripture quotations
are taken from the HOLY BIBLE, NEW INTERNATIONAL VERSION
Copyright © 1973, 1978, 1984 by the International Bible Society.
Used by permission of Hodder and Stoughton Limited.
All rights reserved. 'NIV' is a registered trademark of
the International Bible Society.
UK trademark number 1448790

Cover design by Sam Redwood
Typeset by Temple Design
Print Management by Adare Carwin

Printed in Great Britain by J. H. Haynes & Co. Ltd., Sparkford

Contents

THE AIM OF THIS STUDY GUIDE

The aim of this study guide is to help bridge the gap between the Bible world and our own. Michael Baughen's exposition of the great Biblical themes of covenant and grace has vibrant meaning for us as believers in the 21st Century. The questions that follow help relate the principles he draws out to our own lives and situations. You can use this guide either for your own devotional time with God or as part of a group. Enjoy your study!

USING THIS BOOK FOR PERSONAL STUDY

Begin by praying and reading through the passage and commentary a number of times before looking at the questions. You may find it helpful to note down your answers to the questions and any other thoughts you may have. Putting pen to paper will help you think through the issues and how they specifically apply to your own situation. It will also be encouraging to look back over all that God has been teaching you!

Talk about what you're learning with a friend. Pray together that you'll be able to apply all these new lessons to your life.

USING THIS BOOK IN SMALL GROUPS

In preparation for the study, pray and then read the passage of Scripture and commentary over a number of times. Use other resource material such as a Bible dictionary or atlas if they would be helpful. Each week think through what materials you need for the study – a flip chart, pens and paper, other Bible translations, worship tapes?

At the top of each chapter we have stated the aim – this is the heart of the passage and the truth you want your group to take away with them. With this in mind, decide which questions and activities you should spend most time on. Add questions that would be helpful to your group or particular church situation.

Before people come, encourage them to read the passage and commentary that you will be studying that week.

Make sure you leave time at the end of the study for people to 'Reflect and Respond' so they are able to apply what they are learning to their own life situation.

Introduction

The man started digging . . . the hole became deeper, until he was down thirteen feet. 'We are in with a chance,' said Robert Potter, the architect, standing alongside me there in Riding House Street, London. The hole was by the wall of All Souls, Langham Place.

We urgently needed a meeting hall and had been frustrated in our search for a site nearby. The BBC was one side and the St George's Hotel the other. Neither was going to sell! One day someone said to me: 'Why don't you build your own bargain basement?' I was stunned at the idea. It had never occurred to any of us. The words were prophetic. We had the dig.

Next we needed to have digging inside the building alongside one of the Corinthian columns. It was then that the huge foundations were found. John Nash, the original architect, had built colossal inverted arches linking the church's Corinthian columns together, and then had filled the space with earth. The possibility was clear. Remove the earth and there would be space for a hall. The engineering challenges were considerable but there was no doubt about the strength of these foundations. They were so wide and strong that they had withstood a landmine which had destroyed the St George's Hall next door and severely damaged the church's superstructure. The foundations had not moved.

Our younger son, Andrew, did a history project at school on John Nash (as he literally had inside knowledge). He discovered that when Nash was building the elegant terrace of houses facing Regent's Park, one of the houses collapsed into a pile of rubble. Nash found that the builder had not built proper foundations. So next year he made sure of the foundations for All Souls Church, crowning his Regent Street. The building would be damaged and altered across the years but the foundations would remain secure.

The covenant of God, with all its love and grace, is such a foundation.

What is a biblical covenant? It is not a contract between two parties (although it is close to that at Sinai) but an offer guaranteed by the promise of God, usually requiring only our acceptance or rejection. Although it was, as we will see, a term used with Noah and everybody on earth in the early chapters of Genesis, the actual start of the covenant family of God began with Abraham. Across the Old Testament years the superstructure was built, developed, damaged and almost destroyed but the covenant foundation remained secure.

In the New Testament we see the covenant being fulfilled by our Saviour and Lord, sealed as the New Covenant in his shed blood, guaranteed by his word of promise. It is wonderful to know that he does not require works and deeds as a condition of receiving us but that we can come within that covenant by faith alone, through grace.

Our assurance thus rests on him alone and not on ourselves.

As we trace the development of God's covenant love to his people through this book, I hope you will find it as exciting as I do and be greatly encouraged in your life as one of God's covenant people today – people of grace – grace triumphant!

Michael Baughen

Foreword

It is no exaggeration to say that 'grace' and 'covenant' are two indispensable words in a Christian's vocabulary, and that without an understanding of them – especially in relation to each other – our Christianity is bound to be flawed.

Bishop Michael Baughen's aim in this fine book is to reinstate them in our thinking, and to give us an overview of the Bible from their perspective. He begins with Noah and God's covenant with creation, which is still in force. He urges us to be environmentally responsible, and he ends this section with his own eloquent hymn expressing thanksgiving for creation.

Abraham and Moses feature prominently in the next chapters. Through their strategic ministries God's covenant people emerge and develop. Then, when at last the New Covenant dawns, the Bishop positively 'bubbles' (his word!) with excitement over the fulfilment of God's promises in Christ and his cross.

This leads Bishop Michael to issue serious warnings against legalism, as incompatible with our identity as people of grace, and to challenge us to live out the radical ethic of the Sermon on the Mount.

Interspersed with the text are exhortations to his readers – whether individuals or groups – to 'pause and think' or 'pause and pray', and he helps us to do so by supplying us with pertinent questions.

Michael Baughen has put us in his debt by isolating the overarching theme of covenant love and by calling us to live as Grace People: Rooted in God's covenant love.

John Stott

PART A

THE FIRST COVENANTS
OF SALVATION AND GRACE

CHAPTER 1

The Noah Covenant: Why was it necessary?

Aim: To see from what Noah was saved by the grace of God

FOCUS ON THE THEME:
Myrtle, my wife, is into watercolour painting (and so am I, to some extent). One of the surprises has been to discover how a good painting of a sunlit scene is suddenly transformed into a much truer and sharper picture by the addition of strong shadows. The dark makes the intensity of the light far more discernible. Even a border or a frame can make a huge difference. The framework of the Noah deliverance, with its dark shadows of judgement, makes the wonder of God's grace leap from the pages.

Reading: Genesis 6:1-13
Key verses: Genesis 6:5,6

We will start with the shadows. In the making of the covenant with Noah, we see Noah standing as a beacon of light in a fearfully dark world. Look at the description of the world in chapter 6:11-13: the earth was 'corrupt . . . all the people on earth had corrupted their ways . . . the earth is filled with violence'. Go back to verse 5: 'how great the wickedness of the human race, every inclination of the thoughts of the human heart was only evil all the time.' It was not just violent deeds but the inclination to evil . . . nothing to check it. The picture is one of a totally godless society where any rule of law or standards of morality seem to be non-existent.

God had poured out his love in creation, had formed the two first humans in his own image and had provided for them with love, but humans had marred everything. Girls were still beautiful (v. 2) and remain so today. When God saw (1:31) that everything he had made was good, that included humans and although sin would infest the human spirit, there was still beauty on the outside. As things deteriorate, the Lord says (v. 3): 'My Spirit will not contend with human beings for ever'. Then follows the bit about Nephilim. We are used to the evil that can produce, and be increased by, powerful leaders such as Hitler, Stalin, Idi Amin, Pol Pot, Bin Laden, Saddam Hussein. Here in Genesis, the Nephilim may have been such leaders (v. 4). What started innocently seems to have turned sour and then rotten. Humanity is in contention with God. If we dig further there is clearly more to it with the mention of 'sons of God' in verse 2 and we need to turn to 1 Peter 3:19,20 where we are told that the risen Christ 'went and made proclamation to the imprisoned spirits – to those who were disobedient long ago when God waited patiently in the days of Noah while the ark was being built.'

Thousands of years later Paul will write to the Ephesians with a marvellous exposition of salvation, of being saved by grace, of all the benefits and responsibilities of being in Christ. Then he etches in the shadows with considerable impact, for he knows that the battle is engaged in the spiritual realm, although we only see the earthly manifestation of it. He says in Ephesians 6:12: 'our struggle is not against flesh and blood, but against the rulers, against the authorities, against the powers of this dark world and against the spiritual forces of evil in the heavenly realms.' So it seems to have been from the beginning. So it was in Noah's day. So it is now in our present world.

- *Ephesians 6:12-18 urges us to put on the whole armour of God. Think about it and consider how truly you wear that armour.*

- *Do we seek to support what is good in society and join where we can in action and support to expose evil and to challenge the world's plunging moral standards? Or do we just read about it all and think how sad it is? What more can be done locally and nationally by us and by our church?*

- *Do we have a burden to pray as Paul calls us to do in Ephesians 6:18-20?*

It is time for the God's light to shine brightly against the darkness. That light is in Noah, walking in the midst of a corrupt world. He and his family were alone as they 'walked with God' (v. 9). No one else did . . . no one. Elijah, after Mt Carmel, felt completely alone (1 Kgs. 19:10) but he was not alone; there were several thousand others who did not bow the knee to Baal, as God gently reminded him. We too may sometimes feel alone when we see corruption or godlessness around us, but we are not alone . . . there are millions with us in the family of God and vastly more already home with our heavenly Father. Noah and his family had no such privilege. They were truly isolated except that they had God, like us, and so were never alone.

It is remarkable that Noah could know God at all in those days. He stood out (v. 9) as 'a righteous man, blameless among the people of his time'. Nowadays Christians and Christian families may be the only ones walking with God in their street or workplace or school or youth club. It will be evident to others. Christians will need to stand against peer pressure that wants to make them conform to the world's standards; it may seem a lonely path. So think of Noah. He had this priceless fellowship with God. So do we.

Like Noah, it is our walk with God that keeps us sane. It is the regular talking with him, thinking on Scripture with him and desiring day by day to live righteous lives, which enables this relationship to grow. Our souls are then garrisoned with peace, whatever happens around us. Unlike Noah, we can also usually have the inspiration, support and feeding on God's Word that is part of our church family life.

Fiona Castle tells how she tried to fulfil righteous living with regular churchgoing and great care for others but had no peace. It was only when a friend helped her to trust Jesus and reach out to him that the barriers fell and the flood of God's love engulfed her . . . all inside one hour. Roy said that when she returned after this hour it was like the whole house having been redecorated as the transformation was so dramatic. Her relationship with Christ had begun and it has developed wonderfully in her influential Christian life.

Although the sin-sick world needs our ministry, our involvement with care, evangelism and participation, the holding of a personal walk with God day by day is vital to our spiritual survival. What an amazing privilege it is, to walk with God, to be called his children and his friends. I loved the sign on a Californian freeway: 'You are a child of God; please call home'.

● *If you are reading this alone, stop and consider your relationship with God in Christ. Is it real? Is it developing? Is it a daily walking with him and meditating on his Word?*

- *If so, great! If not, stop right here and seek help. It will transform everything.*
- *If you are reading this as a group: share what this relationship means to you, how it started or developed and whether it is becoming formalised or more personal? Dare to be honest, not least if you know that this relationship has not yet happened.*

In Genesis 6, we see God exercising justice. It was done with a sad heart. God is not a vindictive God but a God of mercy and patience (as we will see later on in the covenant developments through the Bible). Yet in the end justice must be seen to be done or right and wrong cease to have meaning. 'The LORD was grieved that he had made man on the earth, and his heart was filled with pain' (v. 6) – it still saddens our Lord. Here is the deep disappointment of God in the human race, so soon after its beginning. Thousands of years later Jesus would weep over Jerusalem because the people of that city resisted God. Judgement is the last resort for our God who is a God of love and mercy. He longs for people to turn back to him before it is too late. In Noah's day they had plenty of time as he built the ark. As we saw in 1 Peter 3:20, God 'waited patiently'.

God decides on the radical action of a new start for the world (v. 13): 'I am going to put an end to all people, for the earth is filled with violence because of them'. This was not a quick judgement but the climax of increasing pain and despair. So it must be with those who reject him year in year out, and especially those who once professed the faith.

- *Do we share God's pain of heart over those who reject him? Stop and pray for those specifically known to you who reject God. As we pray perhaps for years and years, may we have God's patience too.*

The roar of the helicopter's engines fills the air. It is responding to a SOS call from a sinking freighter caught in a terrible storm. It eventually reaches the freighter and manoeuvres into position, in spite of the raging seas and wind. The ship's crew hang on to anything they can as they wait expectantly on the deck. The winchman is lowered until he touches the deck and stands with them on the heaving vessel that is breaking up around them. He carries the first person back up and then the next and then the next. As each man is lifted off the deck he knows he has been saved from destruction and will be brought safely home. Only the captain refuses to come. He goes down with the ship.

There would be no reason to use the word 'save' if the ship had not been about to sink. There would have been no need for Noah and his family to be saved if the world around was not about to be destroyed. There would be no need for Jesus Christ, the Son of God, to come into the world to save sinners if there was no judgement for sin.

In Genesis 6:18 this saving act of God for Noah is confirmed in the first covenant of the Bible. It is the covenant promise of a loving, saving God offered unconditionally by his grace to Noah and his family, and the animals.

Judgement is not a popular theme. Many want to remove it from Christian thinking as it conflicts with their idea of a God of love. They say things such as 'How could a loving God judge anyone? How could he condemn people?' or 'Everyone must end up in heaven, as a loving God would not exclude them' (universalism). As to the idea of becoming apart from God eternally, they would not want you even to mention it. But judgement runs through the Bible to the book of Revelation.

The great and thrilling truth is that judgement is always matched by the offer of salvation. The choice for humans is between life or destruction, as it is in Matthew 7:13,14: 'Enter through the narrow gate. For wide is the gate and broad is the road that leads to destruction, and many enter through it. But small is the gate and narrow the road that leads to life, and only a few find it.' John 12:31: 'Now is the time for judgment on this world' is immediately followed by 'I, when I am lifted up . . . will draw all people to myself.' The powerful preaching of Peter after Pentecost included both aspects as he urged: 'Save yourselves from this corrupt generation' (Acts 2:40).

When Paul writes in Romans 1:18-20 that 'The wrath of God is being revealed from heaven against all the godlessness and wickedness of human beings who suppress the truth by their wickedness . . . since the creation of the world God's invisible qualities . . . have been clearly seen . . . so that people are without excuse' it is followed by the truth of being justified by faith and having peace with God in Romans 5:1. The darkness of Paul's opening chapters is matched by the superb truths of the gospel set out in luminous clarity.

The salvation covenant with Noah foreshadowed the salvation covenant in which we stand through the love of our Saviour. So let us end this chapter by rejoicing in the words of John 3:16: 'For God so loved the world that he gave his one and only Son, that whoever believes in him shall not perish but have eternal life.'

- *Why does salvation not make sense if there is no judgement?*
- *How do we answer those who say everybody will be saved, regardless?*

FURTHER STUDY

Judgement is not, of course, just an Old Testament concept but is New Testament too. You may like to explore this further, looking up judge and judgement in a Bible Concordance. Or you may like to look at these selected passages on judgement: John 5:22, 5:30; John 12:31; John 16:8, 16:11; Hebrews 9:27; Matthew 12:41,42; John 12:47,48.

REFLECTION AND RESPONSE

- Pray for our world, for the society in which you live, and be prepared to bare your heart of pain to our all-seeing and loving Lord.

- There is much we can bring specifically . . . locally, nationally, internationally.

- Pray for the church (which includes yourselves) in seeking to be light in the midst of a crooked generation, for the strengthening of Christians in the media, in positions of influence; for more Christians in those arenas; for schools and youth-clubs, especially church ones.

- Then pray for specific people you know who stand outside God and so under judgement, that they might see God's light and respond to his wonderful free offer of salvation, that God may open an opportunity for you to show them their need and the way to salvation. Ponder again how you can be a better witness, evangelist and setter of standards.

CHAPTER 2

The Noah Covenant: Salvation

Aim: To see the saving of Noah as a picture of eternal salvation by grace

---

FOCUS ON THE THEME:
As a boy I used to sing that there was a way back to God from sin's dark paths and an open door that one might enter. It was vividly true for Noah entering the ark; it is vividly true for us when we respond to the free offer of salvation through our Lord Jesus Christ and enter the ark of God's family for ever. Let us see the Noah story in that light.

Reading: Genesis 6:14-22
Key verse: Genesis 6:18

The first covenant (and every covenant) is all about grace. It was not Noah's idea to build an ark. There were no broadcast weather warnings. It was entirely God's initiative. He gave the warning of the flood of judgement. He gave the command to build the ark. He said 'I will establish my covenant with you, and you will enter the ark . . .' He had to be trusted implicitly by Noah and we presume that Noah had to put up with mockery, objections, even opposition. Yet Noah *did* trust. He believed God to be trustworthy. He was experiencing salvation by grace alone.

However, the story is very busy and the concept of grace can be swamped by the buzz of activity, the finding of all the wood, the huge building operation, the colossal size of the ark, the storing of food, the gathering of the animals and the loading of them two by two. Children love the story. They have Noah's arks as toys; they love loading the animals; there are humorous songs about the ark. A few years ago, Myrtle and I went to see *The Mysteries* at a London Theatre. It was performed by a brilliant South African group. The representation of Noah and the Ark had us all rocking with laughter as Noah and the sons stood behind a piece of blue curtain, which was kept rippling, but Noah's wife refused to come in and sat in her deckchair on shore. Eventually, the sons distract her and then grab her to take her, protesting loudly, into the ark. It was memorable. But, of course, it had no breath of grace about it at all. It entertained but it missed the whole point of the story.

Did you see the film *The Passion*? If so, what were your reactions to it? Were you disturbed, traumatised, moved, or did you feel detached, like an observer? Whatever you felt, you must have longed for the terrible thirty-nine flogging lashes to stop. Did they need to do that? Was it gratuitous violence? When I thought about it later, I realised how easy it is to read about the floggings; it was very different to see them. It has affected my thinking about the cost of the cross for ever. Yet when Myrtle and I came out of the cinema, we both had the same aching frustration that the film had only in passing answered the question 'Why did he allow himself to suffer and be crucified? What is the meaning of the cross?' That this was the once and for all sacrifice for the sins of the world, the supreme and final sacrifice, was barely indicated. The cross was grace, grace, grace all the way. One longed to write across the screen 'he need not have done it' and 'by grace you are saved, through faith'.

● *Are there ways in which the story of Noah could be better*
communicated to children (and adults) to help them get the
real point of the story?

'Grace' is mentioned in 6:8 although some versions have
'favour' and one has 'a pleasure to the LORD', which is a
lovely translation. So Noah found grace in the eyes of the
Lord in verse 8 and this is followed by verse 9: 'Noah was
a righteous man, blameless among the people of his time,
and he walked with God.' He had shown that he meant
business with God. His was no word-only faith but one
lived out in the daily life of a corrupt world. 'Blameless
among the people of his time' feels like a comment made
by his non-believing contemporaries. To my mind this is
the greatest witness that you and I can bring to the world
in which we live. Most conversions are because of the life-
witness of Christians. People see Christ in Christians; they
seldom turn first to the Bible.

Christians in the workplace, with a life of integrity,
whose word can always be trusted, who will give
thoroughness to their work, who have a buoyancy of
peace plus joy, who are not living for more and more
money and who really care for others are a powerful
witness . . . sometimes an uncomfortable one but often a
quietly attractive one. Such integrity with great humility
has been a mark of Dr Billy Graham and his wife, Ruth.
When he came to England for the first Crusade at
Harringay in the mid-1950s, there was a huge advertising
campaign. The press had a lot to say for and against the
coming Crusade (mostly against) and most sent reporters
down to Falmouth so that they could go out in a tender to
board the ship on which Billy and his team were
travelling. They said later that they wanted to find his
faults, to discredit him, but nearly all of them were

knocked sideways by his humility and wrote very different stories from what they had expected. It is surely because of this humble walk with God that he and Ruth have been so used by God. When they came to the Centenary Keswick they both took notes of the speakers and were keen to learn more of their Lord. When George Carey was Archbishop of Canterbury even his harshest critics had to admit that they would never break his integrity. So we stop and learn from Noah that he was: 'blameless among the people of his time'. Then, as New Testament Christians, we could turn to Philippians 2:14-16: 'Do everything without complaining or arguing, so that you may become blameless and pure, children of God without fault in a warped and crooked generation, in which you shine like stars in the universe as you hold out the word of life'.

● *It is a good moment to stop and examine your own lives whether in work or not, whether young or old. Do others see your integrity? Are you blameless? Are you caring? Are you humble? Do you obviously walk with a quiet faith in our Lord and with his peace and joy in your heart?*

● *Are there specific people in history or contemporaries who stand out to you with lives like Noah's?*

It is because of his close walk with God that Noah is told in verses 13 and 14 of the impending judgement, the flood and the ark. So does this mean that Noah earned salvation by his good life? No. His closeness to God before the ark gave the ground for his trust in God. Covenant grace has to be accepted or rejected. You must have turned to God to trust him before you can do that. Here is the dilemma for so many. They have perhaps looked seriously at the faith and their mind begins to see that it makes sense but the actual step of faith is another thing. It can only happen on the basis of what has been grasped of the faith but it seems to be a huge gap to jump. When people want every problem and query sorted out before they take the step they will never take the step. Only when they do take the step does the Holy Spirit begin to enlighten them and change them and most of their queries fade away. It is the step of faith.

I often recommend the book *A Severe Mercy* by Sheldon Vanauken.[1] Sheldon and his wife came to Oxford from the USA as atheists. To their surprise they found that the students they enjoyed being with in Oxford were mostly Christians. They decided that they had never properly examined the evidence for Christianity and so obtained piles of books and set to exploring. The book contains the superb correspondence with C.S. Lewis. Eventually Sheldon gets to the point where he thinks that Jesus may indeed be God but he cannot take the leap of faith. However, he cannot go back either for there is now also a gulf behind him. It had been easy to dismiss Christianity when he thought of it as fairy tales, but now he might be rejecting God. So he takes the leap of faith; he leaps into the arms of God; the new life begins.

That trust has to be there for salvation grace to click in. Noah had that trust. So God could go straight in with the salvation plan. Hebrews 11:7 expresses this powerfully: 'By faith Noah, when warned about things not yet seen, in holy fear built an ark to save his family. By his faith he condemned the world and became heir of the righteousness that comes by faith.'

● *Think over the relationship between faith and righteousness. We are accounted righteous because of our trust in God but righteous living is also a mark of trusting God. The faith factor is well put across in Hebrews 11.*

● *Think about how we can help others move towards the step of faith and then take it.*

In Genesis 7:16 we have that wonderful phrase: 'Then the LORD shut him in.' God's salvation grace contains this glorious security. As Paul says in Romans 8:31: 'If God is for us, who can be against us?' Later in the same chapter Paul speaks of nothing at all being able to separate us from the love of God in Christ Jesus. We recall the words of Jesus as the Good Shepherd caring for his sheep: 'no one can snatch them out of my hand' (Jn. 10:28). We need to proclaim this great truth. Security in Christ for ever is part and parcel of the covenant of salvation.

The real meanings of the Noah Covenant story are often swamped by distractions over detail. 'What does it mean when it says "the whole earth" was flooded?' 'Was it just that region of the world, the known world of the time, or regions yet to be discovered, the Americas and Europe?' Why worry? What matters is the fact of judgement and salvation. 'Was it all the animals in the world or those in the region round about? Could there have been other animals and creatures in other distant parts of the world?' Why worry? Why try to obscure the straight truths here? Noah did not go out to search for the animals. They came to him (Gen. 7:9) . . . perhaps sensing the coming flood as animals did in the tsunami of 2004. They were male and female of every kind; they were clean and unclean; there were sacrificial animals for the eventual sacrifice in 8:20.

Salvation looks forward to the final gathering of God's covenant people in the new heavens and the new earth. Do you recall the hymn which says that God is working out his purposes as year succeeds to year? It speaks of God's glory on earth as waters covering the sea. One of the marks of that time will be the wolf and the lamb living together (Is. 11:6). Was this foreshadowed in the ark?

The waiting day after day after day must have seemed interminable and it must have tested Noah's trust. There had been no promise about survival, only the command to get in the ark. Again, Noah had to trust, not knowing what the outcome was going to be. Trust is often like that. In Hebrews 11 it says of all those who had walked by faith in God: 'All these people were still living by faith when they died. They did not see the things promised; they only saw them and welcomed them from a distance.' In the Christian life some go through times of blackness, of feeling spiritually cold in worship, or of raising queries when suffering and it is then that we must lay hold of the facts. God has promised his covenant grace in Jesus and we have accepted his salvation. That means we are on secure ground, even though our feelings do not sense it. Noah had to trust . . . and trust . . . and trust. So must we.

● *Have you been through times of feeling apart from God? If you are in a group, perhaps others have been through this. Share experiences and how you came out of those bleak times.*

After 150 days came the first hint of the situation changing. Then God 'remembered Noah and all the wild animals and the livestock that were with him . . .' (8:1). The wind came. The rain ceased. Eventually the ark came to rest on dry land. God had fulfilled his covenant promise. Noah and his family had been saved. A new life could begin. The whole experience must have tested Noah's faith . . . and strength . . . and patience, but it was all so worthwhile, and the new life after having been saved would be wonderful.

So let us end this chapter on the thrilling note of our salvation. We can now rejoice in the amazing grace of God towards us in Christ. By grace we are saved – saved from judgement. It is a marvellous truth, a marvellous privilege, a marvellous joy.

We are his covenant people for ever.

FURTHER STUDY

I have frequently quoted 'by grace you are saved, through faith' so you might like to study Ephesians 2 where it occurs (v. 8).

REFLECTION AND RESPONSE

- It could be a help to our personal witness if we learnt from different evangelists (look at their DVDs, videos, books, booklets and pamphlets) how they seek to present the truth of salvation by grace to people of today, including children and young people as well as all ages upwards.

- Do we need different approaches in different social areas? E.g., how do you seek to do evangelism in an area where money is no object and material plenty abounds; and in an area where the opposite is true? Collate some arguments and texts so that you can be equipped with an answer when challenged.

- In your meditations, you might like to ponder again what an amazing privilege it is to have been made God's children through grace and faith, so that death has lost its sting and judgement has been swept aside.

CHAPTER 3

The Creation Covenant: Its dimension

Aim: to grasp more fully the amazing scope of God's covenant promise to humanity

FOCUS ON THE THEME:
The penetrating charge that 'Your God is too small' still remains relevant. We can so easily get into a limited view of God and I find it refreshing and challenging to stop and see God's infinite greatness. Here we see the infinite scope of his Creation Covenant promise.

Reading: Genesis 8:15 – 9:17
Key verses: Genesis 9:8-13

The waters recede; the ground is dry; Noah is instructed to come out of the ark, with his wife, his sons and their wives. All the animals file out as well. They have been saved and are alive. The experience has been overwhelming, physically and spiritually. God has been utterly faithful and the unswerving trust of Noah has resulted in salvation and a new life.

No wonder Noah's first instinct was to give thanks. So it should be for us. If we come suddenly to faith, the praise and gratitude will be spontaneous; if we come gradually, like the dawn, as I did, we need to appreciate what God has brought us from and into, as his children saved by grace, and then we will praise. Noah offered a sacrifice of thanksgiving.

Then comes God's breathtaking, mind-blowing promise in 8:22: 'As long as the earth endures, seedtime and harvest, cold and heat, summer and winter, day and night will never cease.' What a promise as a prelude to the next covenant. It is often read at harvest services and really needs to be read with 'oomph' . . . it ought to make everyone sit bolt upright with its force. Then the amazing scale of the promise needs to be pondered, digested and turned to worship and active response. This was not a promise just to Noah. It is missing the point to head this chapter, as has been done in some Bible versions, 'God's Covenant with Noah'. In 8:22, it is a divine pronouncement in Noah's hearing but not addressed just to Noah. In Genesis 9:9, the promise is given covenant status. It is to Noah, all his descendants (which must mean all humans) and every living creature. Thus it is to the whole world. It includes every atheist as well as every believer. That it includes all animals changes our attitude to them; they are included in the same covenant as we are; they have the same Creator as we do.

The first covenant was with Noah; the second was with all created beings. For the rest of Scripture we see the covenant family start and develop from Abraham to Revelation. So this Creation Covenant is a one-off. It stands alone but it also stands until Revelation and the end of the world. In the songs of heaven in Revelation 4 and 5 we have the two main songs of praise, one to God as Creator and one to God as Saviour.

● *Pause a moment to reflect on the scope of this covenant and to give praise and thanks to God for such an amazing guarantee about his creation.*

H.L. Ellison, a 'fulfilled Jew', was a clear and powerful exponent of the Old Testament as a Christian believer. I had the privilege and immense benefit of sitting under his teaching on the Old Testament. He began the course by leaning across the podium and saying, in his penetrating accent, 'The trouble with you Gentiles is that you think the Bible began at Matthew 1 and not at Genesis 1.' By the end of the course you would never think that any more.

There is a vast amount of grounding for our Christian faith throughout the Old Testament. For a people so often living in the open spaces, with the expanse of the heavens above them, it is not surprising that there is much to teach and inspire us about God as Creator and the wonder of his creation. Those of us living in towns and cities may not be stimulated as readily so we need the Old Testament to keep blowing open the dimensions of our dependence on our Creator Lord.

Bishops in the House of Lords are responsible for saying prayers at the start of each day's session. There is a set choice of psalms. I loved using Psalm 24 and letting it rip around the Chamber: 'The earth is the LORD's, and everything in it, the world, and all who live in it' and especially 'Who is this King of glory? . . . The LORD Almighty – he is the King of glory.' It often elicited an appreciative response. Whatever would be debated over the following hours and whoever said it, we needed the dimensions clearly set as people under God.

We see it in terms of trust in Psalm 121 where the eyes are lifted to the hills and the question is asked 'Where does my help come from?' Then comes the emphatic answer 'My help comes from the LORD, the Maker of heaven and earth.' This is the true dimension of faith. We stumble and doubt if we make God too small.

In 1 Chronicles 29:11, when the gifts are brought for the building of the temple, David exclaims: 'Yours, O LORD, is the greatness and the power and the glory and the majesty and the splendour – for everything in heaven and earth is yours.' Spot on, David! He was tackling a vast project in the building of the temple but its apparent vastness shrank in the light of God's creation majesty and power. Remember the children's song that tells us our God is a great big God.

● *Pause to think of other Old Testament references to God as over all things, Creator and Sustainer of the universe. To start with, look at Psalms 2; 8; 29, and so on.*

The New Testament takes us further in this scope of God's power, authority and sustaining of the whole universe. John 1:3,4 says of Christ: 'Through him were all things made; without him nothing was made that has been made. In him was life, and that life was the light of all people.' Notice the two uses of 'all'. Nothing and no one is excluded. The atheists may hate the idea but it does not alter the fact that they are included.

In the incident of the storm on the lake in Luke 8:22 we see this theological truth, in a scene to which we can relate, as the disciples say: 'Who is this that even the winds and the water obey him?' As we face rough seas in life, it is a truth to grasp firmly. In Colossians 1:15-17 the whole gospel is rooted in who Jesus is and it is creation that is the basis of the declaration: '[The Son] is the image of the invisible God, the firstborn over all creation. For in him all things were created; things in heaven and on earth, visible and invisible, whether thrones or powers or rulers or authorities; all things were created by him and for him'. Again, absolutely nothing is excluded. Yet when we start to think of the scale, with the Milky Way galaxy having 100 billion stars or being 100,000 years across, with the universe being at least ten billion light years across, we need to re-read those verses to try and take them in and so enlarge the dimensions of our faith and understanding.

The letter to the Hebrews also wants us to be absolutely clear as to who Jesus is and to see the creation dimension of his person, before it goes on to talk about the cross. In 1:2 we read of Jesus: 'through whom he made the universe'. Verse 3 says he is 'sustaining all things by his powerful word' and then in verse 10 we are shown that not only did he lay the foundations of the earth and that the heavens are the work of his hands but that one day he will bring them to an end (v. 12): he will roll them up 'like a garment' and that (v. 11) though they will perish, he will remain.

These are such heartening passages of Scripture when we look out on the disturbed world in which we live. I have quoted them to underline the point that the promise of the covenant in Genesis 9:8-11 is made by the same God as we see in the rest of Scripture and especially in the quoted passages. He has the right to make this promise. Yet it is entirely one of grace, like every covenant. There are responsibilities and requirements for humankind, as we will see in the next chapter, but not conditions.

● *Pause a moment to ponder the passages we have looked at, perhaps to ask forgiveness for small thinking about God, perhaps to revel afresh in the truths and to offer up praise and worship to your Creator Lord as Lord of all things and giver of this promise to all humanity and animals.*

We have a superb evangelistic tool in these truths. When I talk to sixth formers in schools the questions about God or no God often spring from a basic assumption that Genesis is rubbish or that science has disproved the Bible. It is such a block in their ears (and the ears of much of the population) that until we try to tackle it, they will not hear the gospel. Paul took this approach with those who thought themselves the intellectual elite in Athens when he spoke on Mars Hill in Acts 17. In verses 24 and 25 Paul says: 'The God who made the world and everything in it is the Lord of heaven and earth . . . he himself gives everyone life and breath and everything else.' His method was first to compliment them on being religious, and then to declare their religion 'ignorant'. After that he throws down the gauntlet about God as Creator of all, calls for repentance and speaks of the resurrection of Jesus as proof. Now some will say he was not very successful in this approach. That would be too hasty. Elsewhere he faced the bigoted closed-in thinking of Jewish leaders but here he is entirely in the secular environment and only the dynamite of God's revelation by his Spirit will break through. Our part is to declare the truths of God. They will more often than not be repulsed but sometimes seeds are sown.

I will nearly always use Genesis 8:22 in that environment and throw down the challenge. 'How could anyone dare to write at the beginning of history that "as long as the earth endures, seedtime and harvest, cold and heat, summer and winter, day and night will never cease"? Would anyone dare to write that even today?' If it was fabricated by a human being rather than being a promise of the Creator God, it could have been a faith-destroyer, if it had not been fulfilled. But it has been fulfilled. There is enough food in the world if we can get it to where it is needed. The earth has not gone off its axis; year has succeeded year; season has followed season. As in Hebrews, it is from here that we can go on to the way the same God has acted for our salvation in the person of Christ.

It would be useful to have learnt facts and arguments from books on God and the universe. Professor Russell Stannard powerfully uses the account of the incredible sets of circumstances that had to happen for carbon to be created (necessary to make living creatures). Fred Hoyle, the archetypal atheist scientist, was so shaken when he discovered the near-impossibility of that carbon-making sequence that he would speak of 'him who fixed it' but not say 'God'! There are many excellent contemporary books to strengthen our armour and to sharpen our sword.

The creation-covenant in Genesis 9 is a penetrating argument to unbelievers. As we press home the fact that everything they have – life, breath, food, and so on – is dependent on the sustaining of the universe by God, we may receive a blunt disagreement but, as we pray, the truth might still get through their armour and begin the opening of their heart to seek the Lord.

- *If reading this in a group, discuss the use of this covenant truth in witness, apologetics and testimony. Share books or articles you have found helpful or tell of experiences in trying to witness from this base.*

- *If alone, ponder how you can prepare yourself better to speak of this amazing covenant promise; perhaps put a note in the diary to go to a Christian bookshop to get helpful books on the theme.*

The rainbow is the sign of the covenant promise in 9:13. It is a sign to everyone, whereas signs of the other covenants are to believers and more intimate. Of course, the rainbow existed already but was now invested with this meaning until the end of the world. Everyone loves a rainbow. We can all recall its fascinating beauty lifting eyes and hearts in a humdrum setting or thrilling us when seen in full view in the wider landscapes or seascapes. The word for rainbow means 'bow of a warrior' and it seems to indicate that God is hanging up his bow about creation until the end of the world, so underlining the covenant promise.

The rainbow is another way in to speak to non-believers and again, even if they dismiss what we say, they will keep seeing rainbows and results may eventually come in their lives. For all of us, as believers, it should be a moment not only of gazing with excitement on the spectacle but also of lifting our hearts to our glorious Lord with praise and thanksgiving for the wonderful covenant promise of Genesis 9.

FURTHER STUDY

The more we start to think about this covenant, the more interesting, exciting and mind-opening it will become. You could research more fully in Scripture or get into specialist books (see the end of chapter 4).

REFLECTION AND RESPONSE

- Get a large sheet of paper and begin to jot down all that you can think of about your own life as a created being and all the wonders and resources God has given the world and on which we depend.

- Keep the list handy and keep adding to it day after day.

- Then go through the list line by line, giving thanks to God for everything.

The Creation Covenant: Responsibility

Aim: To consider the responsibility for the environment expected from us by God

FOCUS ON THE THEME:
How seriously do we take the matter of creation and the environment? Top of our Christian agenda will no doubt be salvation, evangelism, church growth and Christian holiness. Creation seldom gets a look in, apart from at harvest and perhaps once or twice at some other times of the year for most churches. Yet it is clearly high on God's agenda.

Reading: Genesis 9:1-7; Genesis 1:28-30
Key verses: Genesis 9:7; 1:28

God's declaration that never again will all life be destroyed by the waters of a flood in 9:15 is an amazing act of grace, considering the mess humans would make of the world. It is unconditional and undeserved. It is for ever. The flood is a demonstration for all time of judgement on a sin-ridden world. The statement in Genesis 9:15 is a demonstration of abounding mercy.

Before we go any further, let us pause to see this as an example of handling the tension between judgement and mercy. James 2:12,13 warns us about judging without mercy and declares 'Mercy triumphs over judgement!' Jesus shows us his handling of this tension in John 8:1-11 with the woman caught in adultery. Judgement is called for by the Pharisees and this meant death by stoning. Jesus suggests that any person without sin should cast the first stone. So the woman is spared. Yet he still tells her to go and sin no more. There is no hiding the sin, but he is quicker to show mercy than judgement.

In the Sermon on the Mount he warns us (Mt. 7) against judging lest we too are judged. He suggests that we may find that it is only a speck in the eye of the person we are judging but that there is a plank of wood in our own. It is so easy to make judgements, isn't it? We easily do it by attributing motives to someone's actions and not trying to discover the real motives which may be very different and would elicit understanding. In my second curacy Sundays were extremely busy. Not only was there the early Holy Communion services but then there was the 10 a.m. Covenanters Bible Class for boys held in the cemetery chapel alongside the church. By the time that had finished there were usually only three or four minutes for me to get to the church vestry, change, and process in for the 11 a.m. service. I ran every time. One day a Church Councillor gave a judgement on me to the Council, saying I was inefficient and lazy for not getting to the church early: he was certain about this because he saw me running. That is a simple example but so often it can be far more serious. Love and mercy hesitate to judge until all is known.

Even then, mercy must be involved. When I was a boy at school I learnt a practical lesson in this. Some other boys and I saw a loaded apple tree in the garden of an empty house, en route to school. We decided to get some of the apples. We were caught red-handed by a neighbour. He took all our names and then tore the piece of paper up. Judgement was met by mercy and the lesson powerfully learnt.

I once preached at a civic service on this tension of mercy and judgement and was amazed at the response afterwards from the headmaster of a major school, from the Police Commander and several others in leadership. Being responsible as a Christian and a beneficiary of the Creation Covenant pushes us to working with this tension and always checking ourselves when we are about to make quick judgements.

● *Think through this tension in your own life.*

● *If you are in a group, then this is something that can be helpfully shared together so that you can learn from one another.*

Another tension comes out of this covenant. In Genesis 1:29 God gives humans every seed-bearing plant and fruit-bearing tree for food; he gives animals, birds and other creatures every green plant for food. However, in Genesis 9:3, in the establishing of the covenant after the Fall, God says 'Everything that lives and moves will be food for you. Just as I gave you the green plants, I now give you everything.'

There is no vegetarian agenda here. Humans are permitted to eat flesh. The only restriction is 'you must not eat meat that has its lifeblood still in it' (v. 4). There is a special judgement on animals or humans who take human life. So does this make us pacifists? Is there such as thing as a just war? Should we have let Hitler dominate the world or were we right to fight him and his regime? Is Genesis 9 talking about a personal responsibility whereas resistance to evil is corporate and so different?

What is our responsibility towards animals and all living things, as well as to the environment? There are tensions between having open access to animals and plants for food and the parallel requirement to preserve life and to care for fellow-humans, animals, plants and all living things. For some people, these issues raised here have become a major concern – vegetarianism, pacifism and animal rights all have their supporters in the church. Whatever we think, we need to ensure that our convictions are based on a thorough examination of what Scripture actually says.

God is green! Of course he is . . . he is the Creator. Humanists leap on top of the green issue and in so doing they show us how little we Christians have spoken and acted on the issue in past years. That is now changing. It should have always been high on our agenda, as responsibility for the environment is the consequence of the Creation Covenant of Genesis 9. The Greens accuse the Bible of allowing the rape of the world's resources. They point to Genesis 1:28: 'fill the earth and subdue it. Rule over the fish . . . the birds . . . every living creature'. It is easy to lift this phrase and misuse it. However, 'subdue' is the word for stewardship. It would be less misleading if it was translated 'Be stewards of'. Think of a garden. To make it productive and beautiful it will need work done on it . . . we can readily call that 'subduing' but it is clearly not a permit for the rape of its resources. Stewards are responsible to the Chief Gardener. We act on his behalf to care for and use his creation in line with his intentions and purposes. He has told us we can use it and feed from it.

The sin factor is the greed, the irresponsible actions such as destroying the rain-forests which we are doing, I am told, at the rate of 78 million acres a year. Burning fossil fuels as much as we are doing is irresponsible and is leading to global warming and violent climate changes. But many countries refuse to take any notice because they are more concerned about protecting their economies. As a race we have been irresponsible stewards. All of us are now being affected. The devastation, if the sea-level rises and causes vast areas of land, even whole countries, to disappear, is a prospect of the utmost seriousness. Failure to be sufficiently concerned to take action is a sin against the Creator.

● *Many issues have been raised in this chapter so far. You may like to pause in order to think through them or you may prefer to do so at the end of the whole chapter.*

How can we respond? Firstly, I believe we need to acknowledge our sin as Christians in not being sufficiently concerned with the proper stewarding of creation – the creation so beautifully provided for us by God. With that repentance, there needs to be the taking up of a positive and practical agenda individually and as churches on green issues. It is not enough to say we are so busy evangelising and being church that we cannot cope with this as well. It is a charge on humankind and that obviously includes us. It is also an arena where Christians can be alongside non-Christians in action and may well break down barriers to the gospel. As we share in environmental action and care we do so with the special sense of responsibility towards our Creator God as his stewards as well as in love to our neighbour, and with concern for the world.

Secondly, we should seek to encourage all responsible development in the world. Creativity is part of our being made in the image of God. Humans have been amazing creators but, more often than not, they never see their creativity as part of their God-given being. We live with so many wonderful benefits these days and are constantly amazed at the resources God has provided in his wonderful creation, which humans can discover and with which they can invent. This is an opportunity for pre-gospel witness. We praise those who have been brilliant in discovery, invention and so on but let us also loudly praise the Creator who gave them creativity. At the same time we see how creativity can be abused and used contrary to the Creator's intentions.

Thirdly, we must not cease in our care and concern for the many parts of the world suffering through war or earthquakes or drought. Christians have often been in the lead in this or, at least, as major partners in relief operations. It does need to be responsible care. Taking lorryloads of things to a poor country may seem to be a caring thing to do but if the contents are not what the people need, it is mere 'do-gooding'. We do need to be certain about the needs before we act. It is also great that we have not confined our care to Christians.

During the Bosnian conflict, Myrtle and I went out to Herzegovina representing Operation Christmas Child – the original shoebox enterprise. All the aid being brought there was to Muslims. They knew we were Christians and welcomed us with great joy and gratitude. We gave out the shoeboxes of gifts and we gave Easter eggs. It was love in Christ's name from OCC, even though the local people regarded the symbol of the cross as the sign of their Bosnian Serb enemy (so we did not wear it). They had almost nothing. Their shops and banks were empty; they lived under daily shelling; yet they responded to love. Myrtle and I were very thankful for OCC's truly Genesis 9 love in the name of Christ. We have seen the same love in southern Albania, with one church in Sarande caring for families in need even though the families do not come to church services. Such is their care and integrity that in the Kosovo conflict the government asked them to care for five thousand Kosovan refugees. Again their love as Christians embraces the Genesis covenant responsibility.

Fourthly, we can do our bit in responsible conservation. We should walk instead of driving when we can, re-cycle paper and bottles, turn down our central heating, use less water and so on. These things are small in effect but not if millions do the same.

● *What about the encouragement of art and music in schools? Should experiments on animals be supported (if so, under what conditions) or not? What about the way animals are reared or transported? Is it right to join in protest marches to persuade international summits on the environment to act more radically?*

Finally, we do not swerve from believing that a converted person who has come into a personal relationship with the living God through Christ can have, should have, must have a far greater sense of responsibility to the world than an unbeliever. So evangelism is our priority, to bring people to Christ, with all that this gloriously involves, but this should lead to our becoming more caring and more responsible as God's stewards for his wonderful creation. Eventually (Rom. 8:21) 'the creation itself will be liberated from its bondage to decay and brought into the glorious freedom of the children of God.' Until then the Creation Covenant of Genesis 9 demands our trust and our responsible action.

FURTHER STUDY

The number of Christian books on this theme is increasing all the time, e.g. the superb books by Professor John Polkinghorn or *Jesus and the Earth* by Bishop James Jones[2] and the one edited by Russell Stannard, *God for the 21st Century.*[3] We may not always agree but our thinking will be stimulated.

REFLECTION AND RESPONSE

• I am sure that you will want to pause to give yourself a thorough check-up on your attitude to God's creation and created beings.

• Then think through what practical steps you might take in your home and in your daily life to play a fuller part in conservation and care.

APPENDIX

A HYMN OF THANKSGIVING FOR GOD'S CREATION

1. God, creation comes from you,
   praise and glory are your due;
   through your Son all things were made
   and your splendour is displayed.
   thank you for the nights and days
   for the stars on which we gaze
   sun to warm and give us light
   moon to keep earth's rhythms right.

2. Earth proclaims your mighty hand
   in the air and sea and land –
   deserts, forests, rivers, lakes
   fertile plains and mountain 'quakes;
   for the life-forms that abound
   for the joys of light and sound
   for the wonders that amaze
   we now bring our heartfelt praise.

3. For the trees that clean our air
   give the nest, the perch, the lair
   flowers of beauty, nectar sweet.
   fruit and vegetables to eat.
   For all animals, our friends,
   on whom much of life depends
   giving friendship, transport, food
   working with us for our good.

4. For the frogs and butterflies,
   birds of beauty in our skies,
   ants and apes and yaks and hares
   horses, donkeys, polar bears;
   For all fish within the sea,
   for the chicken, cow and bee,
   for the eagle, sparrow, dove,
   for the dogs and cats we love.

5. You created humankind
   gave us body, spirit, mind
   breathed in us your living breath
   promised life instead of death;
   when we sinned, you came to save;
   Jesus Christ, your Son, you gave;
   dying for us on the cross
   bringing victory out of loss.

6. We have harmed the world we're in,
   Lord, forgive us for our sin;
   teach us all your gifts to share
   that the poor may not despair.
   then, as children of new birth
   in new heavens and new earth
   we will worship, hearts ablaze,
   joining in creation's praise.

(© words: Michael Baughen. 2005. Jubilate Hymns.)

Tune: St George's Windsor (*Come you thankful people come*) or
Holy child with repeat of first four lines of verse 1 as finale.

PART B

THE BEGINNING OF
GOD'S COVENANT PEOPLE BY GRACE

CHAPTER 5

Abraham: The foundation covenant

Aim: To see the Abraham Covenant as the start of God's eternal covenant purposes

FOCUS ON THE THEME:
Not only is this covenant the key to the understanding of being covenant people throughout the Bible right through to today, but it also establishes basic covenant principles such as faith, grace and relationship to God.

Reading: Genesis chapter 15
Key verses: Genesis 15:6 and 15:18

When I married Myrtle I found that her family was very large, with numerous uncles and aunts. It was a necessary and delightful task to get to know them. For many people today, researching the family tree has become an enthusiastic pursuit. In the same way, new Christians coming into the Christian family ought to visit the family's portrait gallery, to be introduced to Uncle Abraham, Auntie Sarah, Uncle Moses, Auntie Deborah, Uncle David and so on. Abraham is top of the list. Although the covenants with Noah and with the whole world via Noah are important, the actual covenant family, to which you and I belong through Christ Jesus our Saviour, began with

Abraham. He is our many times great-grandfather in the faith. As such he not only laid the foundation stone of the family but he also established its basic framework and characteristics.

In Genesis 12:1-4 God calls out Abram and gives the promise of blessing to all the peoples on earth. It is THE Mission Statement of Scripture, so powerfully fulfilled in our Lord Jesus Christ.

So it is really no surprise that when Peter is out on the streets of Jerusalem after the Day of Pentecost, he explains the healing of the lame man in this way 'The God of Abraham, Isaac and Jacob, the God of our fathers, has glorified his servant Jesus' (Acts 3:13). The link is seamless for Peter. He then throws down the gauntlet with his powerful account of the cross and follows this up with a further covenant punch, arguing that this coming of Christ was foretold and expected. The covenant link is spelt out (Acts 3:25): 'You are heirs . . . of the covenant God made with your fathers. He said to Abraham, "Through your offspring all peoples on earth will be blessed."' He sees Jesus as fulfilling this promise and coming first to the Jews to bless them.

Stephen, in his powerful speech that led to his martyrdom, similarly links the coming of Christ to the 'God of glory appearing to our father Abraham' (see Acts 7:2).

● *You may be very well acquainted with Abraham, your most senior family relative, but there is always more to see and learn from re-studying the chapters about him. If you are only hazily acquainted then resolve to get into the family portrait gallery and especially to get 'into' Abraham.*

There are several basic marks of covenant people which we see in Abraham:

1. OPENNESS TO GOD

'The word of the LORD came to Abram in a vision' (Gen. 15:1). What does this mean? What was the vision? an angelic announcement? an inner conviction?

Have you had a vision? Have you seen the Lord or an angelic messenger at the end of your bed? Very few have that experience, although there are some – including the initiator of the Melanesian Brotherhood in the Solomon Islands. He was clearly a chosen leader for God's mission in those islands but he turned his back on God's call and joined the police. Years later, as a police sergeant, he fell when chasing someone and ended up in hospital, unable to move. He says that Christ appeared to him and said 'Why did you disobey my call?' He surrendered himself there and then and was able to get out of bed and start the immensely effective evangelism of the Melanesian brotherhood. However, if we demand it as proof, for instance, of God's calling to us we will probably be disappointed. Such an expectation may cause us to be blind and deaf to the powerful conviction within us that is actually his call. In Isaiah 6, Isaiah has an overwhelming vision of the glory of God but his call comes by his overhearing God say, 'Whom shall I send? And who will go for us?' God did not call Isaiah by name but he first opened him up to the divine glory and then Isaiah became attuned to God's voice. That openness was the key and the vision stimulated it.

It is a desire to be open to God that is the key. It must have been such a desire in Peter's heart when he went up to his house-top to pray and had the powerful vision of clean and unclean animals to teach him to be open to the Gentiles. It is no surprise that God gave the vision of the future to the aged apostle John on the island of Patmos, as John walked so closely with him and would have had the space and time in exile to wait upon God in prayer and meditation. It could only be a person open to God, as Paul was who could realise that God had closed doors and brought him to Troas where he saw the vision of the man of Macedonia, calling him to Europe.

Being open to God is an essential part of *our* life as covenant people. In this mobile, literate, active, non-stop mobile phone calling society there seems almost a fear of quiet. Earphones blast music into the ears with the huge number of tracks on our MP3s or whatever. The TV and computer can be on almost non-stop in some homes. The established idea of a Christian's quiet time each morning is now rare in younger Christians. So much militates against our being quiet with God, letting the dust settle in our minds and walking with God in worship, love, meditation and conversational prayer. It was refreshing to hear a girl in our church say she took a day off from work each month so that she could go into the country and walk with God, to reflect and pray. That would be a great model to follow. God may have burnt twenty burning bushes beside us without our seeing them if we are just 'nose down' to the next activity. Time alone with God is not optional but vital as a member of his covenant family.

Churches must also have this openness. It is necessary for its leaders to get away at least one day a year to wait on God and say 'Lord, what do you want to say to us? What do you want us to do next? What needs changing? What is your plan for our church in your purposes?' Living daily with this openness to God is essential in a Christ-centred covenant church.

Abram received this vision at night as God tells him in 15:5 to 'look up at the heavens and count the stars'. We also benefit from stopping to appreciate the magnificence of God's universe, to see ourselves in perspective, to realise afresh that it is this Creator God who has met us in his mercy and grace, this amazing God who bothers with us individually as his covenant children.

- *How can openness to God as Lord of the church be encouraged more throughout your church family?*
- *How is your own walk with God? Has it faltered or grown 'samey' or is it fresh every morning? Is it a moment to stop to make radical adjustments?*
- *How often do we stop and lay before the Lord whatever we are having to deal with, for his guidance and wisdom?*
- *Are we on the life-path the Lord intends? Whatever our age, it is good that we keep asking God whether we are still in his purpose for us or whether he is calling us to something or somewhere new.*

2. FAITH AND TRUST

Abram believed the Lord, and he credited it to him as righteousness (Gen.15:6)

This needs to be in fluorescent colour or in some huge flashing format to emphasise its foundational importance. It is the first time that a person is spoken of as 'believing' in God. It is the key to the gospel argument for Paul in Romans 4, Galatians 3 and for James in James 2.

It is faith and trust in God. Full stop. When our God is 'too small' so is our faith. Here in Genesis 15:1 God speaks of himself as Abram's 'shield [and] very great reward.' Abram's response shows he is filled with the sense of God's majesty and power by his using the title 'Sovereign Lord' (vv. 2,8). When verse 6 says Abram believed the Lord, it is belief in a Sovereign Lord.

When we come to God in prayer, is it to a Sovereign God? We need to drop our defences, our smokescreens and our self-centred interests and just come to gaze on God, to adore him, to be awed in his presence, to meet him face to face and to want to be more like him. Our requests can follow, but should always be geared primarily to his will, his way, his purpose and his glory; not to our self-centred wants. It is only then that our faith will grow, deepen and stand the test of circumstances. If we come centred on our wants, as if to a God simply there to do our bidding, we shall be hurt when things do not work out in the way we desire and this may weaken or destroy our faith. Real faith in the true God trusts even when the path is unknown, just as Abram had to do when he stepped out of the security of thriving Ur (Gen. 12:1-4 15:7). Real faith in the true God remains secure even in disaster.

An elderly man brought this home to me. He asked me 'Do you remember at the Keswick Convention, when you were expounding Philippians 4:4, that you repeated several times "Rejoice in the Lord, not in circumstances"?' I did. 'It went through me like a dagger,' he said. 'It ran through my mind all night and for weeks and weeks afterwards. Then one morning my wife was killed outright crossing the road. Although the shock was terrible, those words came back into my mind within the hour and I knew why God had laid them on my heart at Keswick. Although I was mourning I was also able to rejoice in the Lord and not in circumstances.' That is covenant faith. Even though he was heart-broken at the loss of his beloved wife he was enabled to keep his eyes on the Lord, on the one who was her and his Saviour and to trust him for the future.

● *The more fully you walk with that trust in your Lord, the more you will want to deepen your faith. We can never get right to the depths of God but we can get deeper all the time, with every testing and every blessing and through all*

*circumstances. It is a pilgrimage. Would you pause
individually or as a group to look at yourself honestly
about this? Is your prayer life mostly or occasionally self-
centred rather than God-centred?*

● *If in a group, can you share experiences in your life where
your faith has been deepened? If alone, reflect on this in
your own life.*

● *Have you or has anyone you know felt called by God to
step into the unknown, as Abraham was from Ur (Gen.
12:1)?*

3. PROMISES

The third strand of the foundation covenant is that of the
promises of God. Our faith is not in the promises *per se*
but in the God of those promises. This is clearly set out in
Hebrews 11:11: 'By faith Abraham, even though he was
past age – and Sarah herself was barren – was enabled to
become a father because he considered him faithful who
made the promise'.

When we sing about 'standing on the promises' it is
important to underline what follows: 'of God my Saviour'.
A promise is worth nothing if the person who makes it is
unreliable. But God is utterly trustworthy.

The promise of heirs and a nation was first given in
Genesis 12:1,2: 'I will make you into a great nation,' Now
in chapter 15:2 Abram raises a query. How can it be
possible for him to be the father of a great nation when he
is childless and a servant will be his heir? His query is
prefaced by 'Sovereign Lord'. It is very human and we can
relate to having faith and yet wanting to know how God is
going to work out his promise. God points him to the stars
and says: 'So shall your offspring be'. He still has no
explanation; just a reiteration of the promise. Abram is

content and believes. Perhaps this has happened to us when we have queried God. We are just given fresh grounds to trust God but no details of how he will act; and our faith is strengthened.

Then there is the promise of the land. This was mentioned in 12:7 and 13:14. In 15:7 there is another query. This time God does give some detail and Abram must have wished he had not asked. The problems ahead are serious but God seals his promise with an awesome happening, a theophany of fire, as the context for the making of the first covenant with Abram.

● *We New Testament Christians have many promises from our Lord to lay hold of and trust. They call for our faith response. Think of as many promises as you can and rejoice in them.*

FURTHER STUDY

It would be helpful to go back to the beginning of Genesis 12 and to read chapters 12 – 14, so as to recall what happened before the covenant event we have been thinking about in this chapter.

REFLECTION AND RESPONSE

• There are, of course, many ways to develop closeness with God and it is worth spending time in a Christian bookshop to look at books about walking with God.

• There are also retreats and Quiet Days. When someone tells me they could never cope with being quiet, they are probably most in need of it. Letting the dust settle and cutting off mobile phones, so that the busy details of life can recede, begins to get us into a greater openness to God. It becomes a searching, revealing, sometimes uncomfortable experience but it is always uplifting as we walk this privileged journey with him.

CHAPTER 6

Abraham: The extension of the covenant

Aim: To see how God extended his promises and showed what responses he expected

FOCUS ON THE THEME:
Abram was going to experience more and more of God's grace, just as we do after we come to Christ and begin to grow as Christians. He also had his faith put to the test to show that it was not just a word-response but a heart and action response. We may not have such a dramatic test but our faith will be tested by life itself and the same expectations of acting on our faith are upon us.

Reading: Genesis 17:1-8; 22: 9-18
Key verses: Genesis 17:1,2; 22:16,17

There is quite a gap between chapter 15 and chapter 17, but the awesome experience by which God sealed his covenant will still be vividly in Abram's mind. Now God confirms that covenant in 17:2 and adds 'I will greatly increase your numbers'.

Although God had said in 15:4 that a son would come from Abram's body, there had been no more detail. It is only later in this chapter that God says how this will happen. So Abram is still in this arena of having received a promise some time ago but with no evidence of it being fulfilled. Now, in repeating and extending the covenant promise in 17:1, God uses the title for himself of 'Almighty' (El-Shaddai – the God who is sufficient; the Rock). Abram's faith is pushed to go deeper by grasping and focusing on this all-sufficiency of the One who makes the promises.

This view of God is taken on board by Abram and becomes part of the family thinking. In Genesis 28:3 Isaac uses it in blessing Jacob. When God renews the Abraham Covenant to Jacob in Genesis 35:11 he uses it. So does Jacob when, in Genesis 43:14, he sends his sons back to Joseph when Joseph is holding Benjamin, and when, on his deathbed, he blesses Joseph.

This is integral to the covenant family thinking and is passed on to us as New Testament heirs. Recall how Paul, in 2 Corinthians, tackling the theme of suffering head on, speaks of 'the God of all comfort'. Certainly Job thought in those terms. He uses El-Shaddai thirty-one times during his suffering. How often do we pray, 'My God, my all-sufficient God, my Rock'? How often speak to him in suffering as 'the God of all comfort'? Trusting God as the Rock even when our feelings are cold, when questions of 'Why?' spring to our lips and our sense of his presence is absent – *that* is the faith God is calling for in his covenant people. Abram's faith is deepened in this way *before* God tells him how the promise of an heir will be made possible. Our prayers must start with God and not with our problems.

- *Pause to think about the all-sufficiency of our God. Are there other parts of Scripture that underline this?*
- *Do we need to repent for not trusting God even when we cannot understand why something has happened to us?*
- *Are there people you know who have shown this sort of faith in an outstanding way?*

What did Abram do? He 'fell face down' (17:3). Back in chapter 15 he experienced the awesome fire of God but there is no mention of any obeisance. Now he falls face down in surrendering reverence. It is now an awe in the heart and life.

Reverence for God as God is easily cheapened. In some churches I have visited I have wanted to say (and sometimes have said) 'Do you believe in God?' Of course, it seems a ridiculous question until you press the point. What do you do when facing a problem or a challenge as a church – do you discuss it or do you pray? What is happening in the service with all its bits and pieces? Are you worshipping God? What is happening with constant excitement of songs and rhythm? Are you worshipping the all-sufficient God? Where is reverence? Most churchgoers no longer kneel, which is a great loss to reverence, but more important is the kneeling of our hearts, the reverence for God as God; the awe, the praise, the wonder, the trust, the personal relationship (see 17:1 when God says to Abram 'walk before me and be blameless').

● *Is this need for reverence something that needs attention in your life and worship?*

The widening of the covenant promises begins in 17:2 with the words '[I] will greatly increase your numbers'. Then in verse 4 it becomes far wider than the lands mentioned at the end of chapter 15. Now it is: 'You will be the father of many nations.' This is confirmed by the name change from Abram to Abraham in verse 5.

Ab means father; *Rah* means high; *am* means signifies multitude. The new name is a public proclamation. Abraham's using of the new name is effectively a sign of his faith that God will fulfil what he promises. God presses the point by changing from 'You will be the father' in

verse 4 to 'I have made you a father' in verse 5. In other
words, when God promises you can count it as sealed and
done, even if you still do not know how he will make it
happen. 'Trust me' is the implication of verse 6: 'I will
make you . . . I will make you'. What a lesson for us as we
walk by faith and trust day by day.

There is yet another widening. 'Nations' and 'kings'
will come from Abraham (v. 6) and, wider still, it is to be
an 'everlasting covenant . . . to be your God and the God
of your descendants'(v. 7).

- *It is worth thinking through this attitude of complete trust
  in our own lives, past and present, and for the future.*
- *If in a group, the sharing of how this real trust in God had
  to be sorted out in members' lives could be very helpful.*

A new requirement is added to the covenant. Up to now
there has been the expectation of trust in response to grace.
Now this is strengthened with the requirement of
obedience as part of that response. Verse 9: 'As for you,
you must keep my covenant, you and your descendants
after you'. The prophets will later keep reminding Israel of
this. Obedience is now to be shown in the act of
circumcision, an irreversible sign of commitment to God.
In Romans 4:11, Paul describes it as 'the sign, a seal of the
righteousness that he had by faith while he was still
uncircumcised' and so goes on to argue that Abraham is
the father of all who believe. All males in Abraham's
family, including household members who had been
'bought', were to be circumcised. This sign of faith was
also given to children as young as eight days old.
Although too young to believe, they are seen here as part
of the faith of the covenant family.

Now, of course, the sign has moved to baptism so that
females and males are equally marked out as committed in

faith. It is a highly significant act. The prophets warned of those who were only circumcised in the flesh and not in the heart (e.g. Jer. 9:25). We are only too aware, sadly, of those who have been baptised or confirmed and who now disregard true love, faith and commitment to God.

● *Pause to rejoice in your having been baptised and freshly determine to live even more openly as a baptised person.*

A further mark of God's power and the testing of Abraham's faith now happens in 17:15 ff. Sarai (now to be called Sarah) is to bear a son by him. At last, in God's perfect timing, trust is met by the details of how God will perform his promise. Abraham prostrates himself again but this time laughs inwardly and wishes Ishmael could have the blessing instead (17:17,18). Sarah also laughs (18:12) at what seems impossible at her age. God responds in words that have been precious to believers ever since, 'Is anything too hard for the LORD?' (18:14). With God the impossible can become the possible and Isaac is born (21:1–3). The trustworthiness of God's covenant promises are superbly demonstrated. They are entirely by his grace and we are to respond with faith and obedience.

Genesis 22 continues the process of widening the covenant promises, but it happens in response to the staggering faith and obedience of Abraham. What went through his mind when God (v. 2) told him to take his son, his only son, whom he loved, and to sacrifice him? God had proved his trustworthiness in the past and he had performed the impossible in giving him Isaac. God had also made it clear that it was through Isaac that the covenant promise would continue. Abraham must have been caught up in a conflict of mind and heart. In verse 5 he uses the words 'I and the boy' rather than 'son'. Was he trying to distance himself from the awesome requirement laid upon him? Isaac queries where the lamb for the sacrifice is but when his father ties him to the altar, what can possibly have been racing through his young mind? His father had said earlier that God would provide the sacrifice, but that must have sounded like mere words as he lay there. Then came the intervention by the angel of the Lord. That was far enough. His faith was utterly proved: 'Now I know that you fear God'. Like a number of experiences we have as Christians, hindsight is a wonderful thing. We can then see why God withheld his hand but while he is doing it our faith is stretched to the limits.

Now comes the widened promise in verses 15-18. Descendants will be as 'numerous as the stars in the sky and as the sand on the seashore.' But significantly for us today is the promise that 'through your offspring all nations on earth will be blessed'. This is the outward vision of the covenant people blessing the whole earth. In fact, Israel turned in on itself and lost the vision; so tragically do some churches who preach the gospel to those inside and have great worship but no outward vision of mission to the whole world. Christ Jesus our Lord commissioned his disciples and thus the whole church to go into all the world. It must never be a small extra to our programme but a main vision of it. Paul grasped this with a pounding heart and brilliant strategic action. A quick test of how far this is true in a church is to see what portion of giving goes to mission, and whether evangelism is always at the top of the agenda for every church council, deacons' meeting or similar key bodies.

- *Is your church truly outward looking? Does it have a passion for those living around it and for the country and the whole world?*
- *If not, what can you do about it?*

Genesis 15 and Genesis 22 form a rounded view of faith within God's covenant people. Genesis 15 is concerned with the saving faith that alone makes us right with God. Paul quotes Genesis 15 in Romans 4 as a main plank of his gospel argument. Genesis 22 is concerned with a faith that issues in action. James says this in James 2.

Some try to set Paul and James against each other but they are really standing back to back to defend, argue and promote one of these two aspects of the covenant relationship. Nor are they exclusive. Although James encouraged faith he reacted to mere words and no action in so-called believers. He himself worked out the faith in the social deprivation of the poor part of Jerusalem. Paul preached the gospel with power but he wanted the churches to live out the faith in holiness, mission and action, including to the needy of the world, and he led the way in his personal life.

Both would no doubt have known our Lord's words in Matthew 7: 'By their fruit you will recognise them.'

Back in 1974, at the highly significant (in what resulted) Lausanne Congress on evangelism, the final covenant document included the following:

> we express penitence for having sometimes regarded evangelism and social concern as mutually exclusive . . . When people receive Christ, they are born again into his kingdom and must seek not only to exhibit but also to spread its righteousness in the midst of an unrighteous world . . . Faith without works is dead.

REFLECTION AND RESPONSE

Faith without works is dead. So a regular check-up on our spiritual health would be a wise thing to do, setting dates in our diary to do so. It can be alone with God, surveying our life, witness, faith, action and how far our lives show fruit for God. We will need to avoid excusing ourselves and be radical in our self-examination. It could be with a spiritual counsellor or friend who will be honest with us. We can so easily get in a rut. The round of life and church activities can consume us.

CHAPTER 7

Moses: The covenant develops

Aim: To see how God wants his covenant people to be a 'holy nation' (Ex. 19:5,6)

FOCUS ON THE THEME:
Moses was raised up by God not only to lead the people out of Egypt but also to be the one through whom the next covenant would be given. This covenant, made at Sinai, was concerned with rules and guidelines for the well-being of God's people. It was a development of the Abraham Covenant and not a replacement. It was never intended to set off a battle between law and grace although this is what later happened.

Reading: Exodus 19:1-6
Key verses: Exodus 19:5,6

My grandfather enthused me with a love of railways. He had worked for the London Midland Railway for all his working life but it was almost a labour of love. It was catching and I caught it. He did more than that for me. When we went as a family to visit him, I used to curl up in an armchair with his old Bradshaw timetable and for hours and hours make wonderful journeys, changing trains, getting all over the country on imaginary journeys.

He infused me with a love of timetables. I still love
timetables. They can be seen as legalistic. They lay down
definite patterns and operating details but in so doing they
enable the railways to run smoothly (at least, that is the
idea). When you love railways, that makes sense. Love
wants the best for what or whom it loves.

God gave his 'timetables', his laws, through Moses. In
his love, he wanted the best for his people and knew that
they needed laws and guidelines to help them. Yet he never
swerved from the Abraham Covenant of love and grace.
Abraham had faith, faithfulness, obedience, grace and a
close relationship to God. So did Moses. Their roles for God
were different but their hearts burned with the same love.

In Deuteronomy 32 we have the Song of Moses and we
see more of that love. He praises the greatness of God and
then says (v. 4), 'He is the Rock, his works are perfect, and
all his ways are just. A faithful God who does no wrong,
upright and just is he.'

Then in verses 11 and 12, he uses this beautiful picture
of God regarding Jacob: 'He shielded him and . . . guarded
him as the apple of his eye, like an eagle that stirs up its
nest and hovers over its young, that spreads its wings to
catch them and carries them on its pinions'. What a picture
of caring love. It is this love, he is saying, that those who
have disobeyed the law are ignoring; it is this God of love
they are offending, not just laws.

Exodus 2:24,25 shows that it is this caring love that
brought God to raise up Moses. God heard the groaning of
the Israelites in Egyptian bondage 'and he remembered
his covenant with Abraham, with Isaac and with Jacob. So
God looked on the Israelites and was concerned about
them'. Any following of God that lost sight of that love
would be off course.

My mother did not have green fingers. Any plant
brought into our house would wither whether it was

watered or not; talked to or not; placed in the sun or not. One day she brought a small stick in from the garden to prop up a sickly plant. The plant died; the piece of wood took root! It grew into a 40 ft. poplar tree, in the back garden. That is what the law became for God's people. As love motivated them less and less, the law took root and became the one thing that mattered. Legalism swamped the mind and the spirit. The Moses Covenant would be seen primarily in terms of law across the centuries to come. The battle for grace and love to be more important than law would be fought by the prophets and then into the New Testament, especially by Paul. Across the Christian era, legalism has festered with alarming manifestations, as the Reformers knew. Martin Luther knew the burden of trying to please God legalistically until he discovered that we are saved by grace. This battle persists today.

Even though the people of God had been led out of Egypt against all the odds, had been miraculously delivered at the Red Sea and had been amazingly provided for by God, their love still diminished while law increased.

- *Are we affected by legalism today in the church? In my teenage years, there were laws about not drinking, not dancing, not going to the cinema etc. and these pulled the mind away from the focus on God's loving purposes for his children. Are there similar legalistic by-laws today? In the church? In ourselves?*

- *In issues that are clear-cut in God's word but not acceptable to many of our contemporaries, can we demonstrate that God's purpose is love in what he commands? Can you think of specific examples?*

- *Are the love of God and his loving purposes truly our motivations as Christians?*

● *If this focus has been diminishing, go to be alone with
  God, to repent and refocus.*

Before we come to the Moses Covenant it is worth looking
at the Abraham link in the early chapters of Exodus. At
the burning bush, when Moses is called, God introduces
himself (Ex. 3:6) as 'the God of Abraham, the God of Isaac
and the God of Jacob'. It is this same title Moses is to use
when he speaks to the elders (v. 16) but with the addition
of the name 'The LORD – I AM'. When God reaffirms his
commitment to bring his people out of Egypt in chapter 6
he goes further than the names of Abraham, Isaac and
Jacob and speaks of the covenant with them (v. 4) and that
he is acting now because 'I have remembered my
covenant'(v. 5). The covenant soon to be made via Moses is
clearly springing out of and based on the original
Abraham Covenant. It is not replacing it.

As we come in Exodus 19 to the establishing of this next
covenant we see God again speaking of his caring love as
he describes the deliverance from Egypt (v. 4): 'I carried
you on eagle's wings and brought you to myself.' This is
the context in which the promise of the covenant
relationship is given (v. 5): 'Now if you obey me fully and
keep my covenant, then out of all nations you will be my
treasured possession' and the Abraham Covenant's
concept of blessing the whole world and not being in-
turned is spelt out in the next verse (v. 6): 'Although the
whole earth is mine, you will be for me a kingdom of
priests and a holy nation' – words picked up by Peter in 1
Peter 2. The connection between the Abraham Covenant
and the Moses Covenant is seamless, a loving progression
and a purposeful development.

● *Pause a moment to reflect on that wonderful phrase (v. 4):
  'I carried you on eagle's wings and brought you to myself.'*

We may look back to how he drew us to himself (not to religion); to the way he has carried us over the years; to the deep abiding we have in him and he in us.

- *Share testimonies of how God has done all this for you.*
- *Then reflect on that beautiful phrase in verse 5: 'you will be my treasured possession.'*

The initial response of the people in Exodus 19:8 sounds genuine enough: 'We will do everything the LORD has said.' For the moment this was a response to the loving statements and a promise to obey without the detail of what the Lord would require of them. It is easy to say it in such circumstances. When in baptism, confirmation or similar major steps in our Christian life, we are encouraged or scripted to say that we will submit to Christ as Lord, we may be quite genuine in our response, as were the Israelites, but the detail of what that will mean in our life is not usually set out. The test of our commitment will come in the detail.

To press home the seriousness of the coming covenant commitment there is an awesome happening. First (Ex.19:10), the people have to show seriousness by consecrating themselves, washing their clothes and abstaining from sexual relations in preparation for the covenant-making. Then, on God's side, there is the display of thunder, lightning, thick cloud and a very loud trumpet blast. God is a holy God. They are not to treat him glibly or insincerely. The covenant is being made with the Lord Almighty. We do well to take note. We are children of a holy God. We must treat him as God with reverence and awe while at the same time revelling in our relationship to him (by grace) as children to a Father. In Hebrews (Heb. 10:19) we are told that we can enter the Most Holy place by the blood of Jesus – an amazing privilege.

But then in Hebrews 12:28,29, after the reminder of the fire and thunder at Sinai and the new welcome we have in Christ, the writer adds: 'since we are receiving a kingdom that cannot be shaken, let us be thankful, and so worship God acceptably with reverence and awe, for our "God is a consuming fire."'

● *How far does worship in our church reflect this balance of reverence and of personal relationship? Does it need to adjust? If so, how?*
● *Does our own worship reflect this balance?*

In Exodus 20, the Ten Commandments are given; the first four concentrating on our behaviour towards God, thus underlining the relationship we have with him, and then the others looking on our behaviour towards our neighbour, living out God's will for human well-being. They are the framework of a balanced and holy life which, when fired by love for God, brings peace to the heart and is a blessing to others. To say, as some do, that they accept the last six but not the first four sounds reasonable but it effectively removes God from them all and makes the last six merely guidelines produced by humans. This then can result in people sitting lightly to them so that, for instance, coveting is rife in today's materialistic society and seldom frowned upon. We can have a government minister commit adultery and then say he has done nothing wrong. In a later chapter we will reflect on how Jesus opened the commandments and strengthened them, with love permeating his exposition of them.

The seriousness of these commandments is then to be underlined in the people's minds by their being required to make an altar (20:24) and on it to offer burnt offerings and fellowship offerings. When we are met by God in a special way, perhaps in his calling us to follow him or to surrender our lives to his purpose or in a time of worship we may often want to respond in some action as well as in words. I recall a young man of seventeen in a youth group when I was a curate. He knew the Lord but there came the moment when he knew God was calling him in a special way. He immediately brought £73 to me to use for God. The next day his father rang me up with anger (understandably perhaps), demanding I repay the money at once. I said that I would do so if the young man requested it back. I put it to his son. He was adamant that this gift (the whole amount of his savings) was his sacrifice to God to show his glad acceptance of God's call. He went forward into God's calling for him with great fruitfulness.

● *Reflect on the Ten Commandments one by one, thinking about the way you live out their requirements in your life as a Christian and how love is their (and your) root and motivation.*

In chapters 21 – 23, there are mainly social laws but then in chapter 24 there is a serious establishing of the covenant. Aaron, Nadab and Abihu, with the seventy elders, are now drawn in, although at a distance. The leadership needed to show its commitment publicly, just as it needs to do in special moments of church life today. This time the response of the people is to the detail of the commandments which are told to them (24:3) and they say (note they did so 'with one voice'): 'Everything the LORD has said we will do.' After the burnt offerings that follow, the Book of the covenant is read again and this time the people add the words 'we will obey' to their response. The blood is thrown against the altar and then, after the people respond, it is thrown over them. The covenant is thus sealed by blood.

In moments of commitment and dedication it is not uncommon for us, his people to have a fresh sense of God's wonder and power. When I eventually said to God 'Here am I, send me' the darkened room (it was late at night) seemed to flood with glowing light. Here in 24:10, Moses and the elders are given a glorious vision of God. It was a wonderful sign that God was their God and had brought them to this covenant as his people.

FURTHER STUDY

Moses is a hero of mine. By studying him my ministry was transformed. Did I believe in the same God as Moses? If so, nothing was impossible if it was God's plan and will. It is worth studying Moses in full.[4]

REFLECTION AND RESPONSE

Reflect on the promises, commitments and pledges you have made to God and see how well they are being fulfilled and how far they are motivated by love. If there has been a slipping back then repentance is, of course, needed. If all is well, or after repentance, why not consciously renew them to God and re-express your love for him as your Saviour, your Lord, your God.

CHAPTER 8

Covenant love

Aim: To see how God's love for his people and their love in response were both fundamental to the covenant relationship and how this had to be constantly re-iterated in order to challenge their sin and disobedience

FOCUS ON THE THEME:
If a son or daughter living a full and wholesome life, with a keen faith, then begins to slide into wrong company, dropping out of Christian activities, seeming to take God lightly and moving away from Christian morality, it is deeply painful to a Christian parent's heart. There is the agonising dilemma of how far you should try to stop the slide and show its seriousness, while maintaining unswerving love. That was the agonising dilemma the Israelites caused to the heart of God.

Reading: Exodus 32:1-10; 34:6-10
Key verses: Exodus 34:6,7a

If we could have stopped at the end of chapter 7 it would have been a 'happy ending' with that glorious vision of God. You can almost hear great music accompanying it. After the vision, Moses is called up to the mountain top (24:12) where he is to receive the tablets of stone on which the laws and commandments were inscribed. There should have been a praise meeting down in the valley, an on-going joy in the grace and love of God. He had brought them into this wonderful covenant relationship, not because they deserved it but because of his love. It was wonderful.

So it is almost unbelievable that in less than forty days the people started sliding spiritually (32:1). Indeed it was more than a slide; it was direct effrontery to the living God. The moral lapse would follow but it all began with the demand for gods that could be seen and handled, in direct disobedience of the first two commandments. Later in 32:24 we have the most pathetic excuse in history when Aaron says, 'They gave me the gold, and I threw it into the fire, and out came this calf!' The Lord tells Moses (32:7,8) that the people have become corrupt and says: 'They have been quick to turn away from what I commanded them'.

The people deserve judgement and God says that their destruction is the way to restart a great nation for the future. Moses pleads for mercy (32:11-12) and he does so by going back to plead the foundation covenant with Abraham (32:13) from which the current covenants sprang. When he is coming back down the mountain with Joshua, a great noise reaches their ears. Joshua thinks it is the sound of war but Moses realises it is singing. They find shouting and dancing, the people running wild and out of control. Once the people had rejected God they did not bother with the moral laws.

The way of repentance is offered. Moses stands in the camp entrance and says (32:26): 'Whoever is for the LORD, come to me'. Nothing is mentioned about the morals. The primary issue is trust in the living God. The Levites come *en masse* but the later chapter shows that there must have been many others. Three thousand refuse and receive judgement. It is a terrible moment. The issue is not settled in Moses' heart. He speaks (32:30-32) of making atonement, he pleads for forgiveness and even, in his passionate love for his people and God's glory (see also in 33:18), is prepared to be the one blotted out in their place (shades of the cross).

● *It is sometimes unbelievable that Christians can suddenly slide. Why do you think that is? Might there have been a gradual decline in heart-love for God? Were they carried more by the fellowship and church activities than by genuine faith? Had prayer and personal Bible-reading ceased? Are there other reasons you can think of?*

● *What might be done to try and prevent this slide?*

● *Are there warnings that we need to hear ourselves?*

There is a new start. The tablets had been smashed (32:19), dramatically showing the people's sin and disobedience, and now new ones are made (34:4). Before the covenant is remade (34:10) there is an emphatic declaration by God (34:6): 'The LORD, the LORD, the compassionate and gracious God, slow to anger, abounding in love and faithfulness, maintaining love to thousands, and forgiving wickedness, rebellion and sin.'

The word used here for 'love' is pronounced in the Hebrew like 'ches-ed'. It is a key word in the Old Testament. It is the one that theological students not studying Hebrew will often learn to write and use in their answers. It primarily means 'covenant love' and is often translated as 'steadfast love' or, sadly, just as 'love'.

It was used by Miriam in her song after the crossing of the Red Sea (Ex. 15:13) and it is there in the third commandment in Exodus 20 but now it is brought up to an over-riding prominence. Later on in Numbers 14:18,19, when the people rebel, Moses bases his pleading with God on it, using the word twice: 'abounding in love . . . In accordance with your great love'. It is used in Deuteronomy 7:8-12, linking back to 'ancestors', which must mean Abraham: 'it was because the LORD loved you and kept the oath he swore to your ancestors that he . . . redeemed you . . . God, keeping his covenant of love . . . If you pay attention to these laws and are careful to follow them, then the LORD will keep his covenant of love with you, as he swore to your ancestors.'

By the time we get to David and Solomon, covenant love seems to be deeply permeating the thinking of those who faithfully followed the Lord. In 1 Chronicles 16:34, when the ark is brought into the tent that David had made for it, the praise song was: 'Give thanks to the LORD for he is good; his (covenant) love endures for ever.' This seems to have become a constant theme in praise. Solomon uses it when the ark is brought into the temple in l Kings 8:23: 'LORD, God of Israel, there is no God like you in heaven above or on earth below – you who keep your covenant of love with your servants who continue wholeheartedly in your way.' 2 Chronicles 5:12-14 gives us a vivid picture of that event. We are told about all the Levite musicians who were playing cymbals, harps and lyres. That would be exciting enough but then, wait for it, the big sound is added of 120 priests sounding trumpets – a much bigger sound than the seventy-six trombones of the stage musical. Add all the singers to all the instruments and you have one colossal sound of praise music, all combining to sing and support this one refrain: 'He is good; his (covenant) love endures for ever' again and again and again. To crown it all, the glory of the Lord fills the temple and the priests are overwhelmed by the smoke and cannot perform their services. It would have been an event never to be forgotten but, as the music faded, the constant refrain must have gone round and round in the heads of the vast crowd. The whole triumphant event sprang from God's covenant love. When the temple was dedicated (2 Chr. 7:3-6) they said the same refrain but this time they were all kneeling with their faces to the ground and they said the words together in worship.

● *Stop and reflect on what such covenant love means to you and how far it undergirds your worship.*

When I was a choirboy, most Anglican churches chanted at least one psalm in every service. Psalm 136 was one on its own, with twenty-six verses all having the same second part. It seemed odd to do that and it felt endless as we chanted through it. Now I can see how wonderful it is and how the repetition of: 'His (covenant) love endures for ever' or in the Prayer Book version: 'His mercy endureth for ever' powerfully gets across the fundamental truth of covenant love as the foundation for all the history of God's people. Look at it and see how it ascribes to God his greatness and praises him for his creation, his saving deliverance of his people, his guidance and protection, his delivering from enemies, his giving his people the inheritance he promised and his provision of needs. It seems to have been an effective way to teach divine history, with every phrase responded to by acclaiming the covenant love of God. By the end you get an overview of history and a penetrating appreciation of covenant love.

● *Do read it, or parts of it, aloud – even if you are alone. If you are in a group, get someone to be the reader of the first part of each verse and then all to respond in unison. Please add the word 'covenant', i.e. 'His covenant love endures for ever.' By actually doing this the importance it gives to covenant love becomes powerfully felt as well as read.*

Following the history of Israel is a bit like riding a big dipper (not my favourite pastime). One moment you are up and the next you are down. We saw that with the covenant at Sinai and what followed. Now we see it again after the climax of joy and love with David and Solomon. Proverbs 3:3 would have been a timely word: 'Let (covenant) love and faithfulness never leave you; bind them round your neck, write them on the tablet of your heart' but, after Solomon, God's people once again *did* let covenant love leave them. It began to wither, while law and legalism took root. The outward ceremonies went on but without the heart being in them. The prophets could see it all so clearly. For instance, Isaiah (Is. 29:13) expresses God's sadness that 'These people come near to me with their mouth and honour me with their lips, but their hearts are far from me.' Joel 2:12,13: the Lord declares 'return to me with all your heart . . . Rend your heart and not your garments.' In Hosea 6:6 God says: 'I desire mercy (this is the covenant love word), not sacrifice'.

The collapse came. Jerusalem fell. The people of God were taken off to Babylon. They had thought that if they kept up the ceremonies, everything would be all right and God would not let his holy city fall. They had really gone their own way. They had not ignored religion; they had ignored God. In devastation they weep in exile and in Psalm 137 we learn how they hung their harps on the trees saying: 'How can we sing the songs of the LORD while in a foreign land?'

● *Are there lessons here for those going through difficulty, sadness or illness? How can we help ourselves or others to get back to the one unshakeable foundation of God's covenant love for us in Christ from which nothing can separate us? Can you apply it in other ways too?*

With everything destroyed – their homeland, the city of Jerusalem, its buildings, its temple and the structure of empty worship ceremonies, it was possible to see again the original covenant foundations. Jeremiah in 33:10,11 sees the vision of a restored Jerusalem where once again the people will declare: 'Give thanks to the LORD Almighty, for the LORD is good; his (covenant) love endures for ever.' In Lamentations, when misery pervades, there suddenly comes the sparkling assurance, like a pyrotechnic display bursting into the night sky (Lam. 3:22,23): 'Because of the LORD's great (covenant) love we are not consumed, for his compassions never fail. They are new every morning; great is your faithfulness.' They are precious words to us but when we think of the atmosphere of despair in which they were suddenly spoken, they are spectacular and utterly amazing. Daniel grasps the truth too when (Dan. 9:4) he prays: 'O LORD, the great and awesome God, who keeps his covenant of love with those who love him and obey his commands'.

A new beginning was possible if God's people would get their faith firmly back on to the foundation of God's covenant love. What God now offered was a further development of the covenant. It is spelt out in Jeremiah 31:31-37. It would no longer be a national covenant as it had become from Moses. It would be a personal covenant. His people would experience something amazing. The letter of the law would no longer be just strapped to their forehead or held in their hands; God would write his law in their minds and in their hearts. Even more was to happen. They would not need to have priests and teachers to be their intermediaries with God for they would actually know the Lord themselves, and that included the greatest to the least. It must have seemed almost unbelievable to Jeremiah's hearers but as New Testament (Covenant) believers, born again by the Holy Spirit, we know just what it meant.

Once again God's people began to rise out of the depths. Other visions of the future were given to several prophets, especially to Isaiah, Ezekiel and Daniel. God moved events for his purposes. In Ezra 1 God touches the heart of Cyrus, king of Persia, in his first year as king. He declares that God has appointed him to rebuild the temple in Judea. He sends a huge number of Israelites back to Jerusalem. They start work on the temple and it is at the laying of its foundation that we know the people of God are back on track with God and firmly back on the foundation of covenant love. With trumpets and cymbals, with all their voices, they sang to the Lord with praise and thanksgiving (Ezra 3:11): 'He is good; his (covenant) love to Israel endures for ever.' Then 'all the people gave a great shout of praise to the LORD'.

Nehemiah also has covenant love at the centre of his heart. He prays to God as the one who 'keeps his covenant of love' (Neh.1:5; 9:17; 9:32). His life seems to be fired by this love and guided by it as he courageously tackles the rebuilding of the walls and the handling of later problems.

The expectation of the glorious coming of a Messiah began back with David when God made a special covenant with him and his house (2 Sam. 7:16, 28). It was to be an everlasting covenant. Its powerful effect is seen in Psalm 2 and Psalm 110. In the period between the Old and New Testaments this covenant hope was the main cohesive theme. Expectation grew; the Messiah came. The final fulfilment of the Abraham Covenant was about to happen. Christ had come and, by his broken body and shed blood, the New Covenant was to be established, for ever.

FURTHER STUDY

If you have a Concordance, look up the word 'love'. In the NIV Exhaustive Concordance[5] the different words used are given numbers. The covenant-love word (che-sed) is listed as 2,876 and so you can follow more of where it is used. However, this is not the only place to look as it is translated in other ways, one of the main ones being 'mercy'. Alternatively, or in addition, you might like to look up 'covenant' in the concordance or in a Bible dictionary.

REFLECTION AND RESPONSE

• Try writing down all the ways in which God expresses his love to you as a Christian; list also specific moments of that love being manifested to you e.g. by his actions or interventions or guidance.

• Now quietly 'do' a Psalm 136 in praise and prayer, i.e. take each item on your list and after each one say in your heart or aloud: 'He is good and his covenant love endures for ever.' Then, on the same day, as you go out, go down the street, go into work, engage in outdoor pursuits or just sit at home, keep saying those wonderful words.

THE GOD OF ABRAHAM PRAISE

This lovely hymn celebrates Abraham, grace and our Saviour. It could be a lovely way in which to respond to the chapters we have just studied.

1. The God of Abraham praise
   who reigns enthroned above;
   the ancient of eternal days
   and God of love!
   The Lord, the great I AM,
   by earth and heaven confessed –
   we bow before his holy name
   for ever blessed.

2. To him we lift our voice
   at whose supreme command
   from death we rise to gain the joys
   at his right hand:
   we all on earth forsake –
   its wisdom, fame, and power;
   the God of Israel we shall make
   our shield and tower.

3. Though nature's strength decay;
   and earth and hell withstand,
   at his command we fight our way
   to Canaan's land:
   The waters deep we pass
   with Jesus in our view,
   and through the howling wilderness
   our path pursue.

4. He by his name has sworn –
   on this we shall depend,
   and as on eagle's wings upborne
   to heaven ascend:
   there we shall see his face,
   his power we shall adore,
   and sing the wonders of his grace
   for evermore.

5. There rules the Lord our King,
   the Lord our righteousness,
   victorious over death and sin,
   the prince of peace:
   on Zion's sacred height
   his kingdom he maintains,
   and glorious with his saints in light
   for ever reigns.

6. Triumphant hosts on high
   give thanks eternally
   and 'Holy, holy, holy' cry
   'great Trinity!'
   Hail Abraham's God and ours!
   one mighty hymn we raise,
   all power and majesty be yours
   and endless praise!

(Words from a Hebrew doxology, Thomas Oliver and in this version Jubilate Hymns. Words © in this version: Jubilate Hymns, 4 Thorne Park Road, Torquay TQ2 6RX Used by kind permission. www.jubilate.co.uk)

PART C

THE NEW COVENANT OF GRACE

The impact of the New Covenant

Aim: to fill our spiritual lungs with the breath of newness, in its amazing scope, ushered in by the New Covenant

FOCUS ON THE THEME:

The main line train drew into the large junction station. As it did so, the branch line train in the parallel platform began to pull out. All the passengers expecting to get on to the branch line train were forced to wait an hour for the next one, with appointments wrecked as a result. Why did it not wait a minute? Because trains run to timetables, came the reply, and do not wait for connecting passengers. This was legalism gone mad. That is what had happened to the Moses Covenant. It had been turned into legalism rather than being, as at its start, a love-act for God's people. Performing ceremonies, as we have seen, came to matter more than a personal relationship with God. So God had to act with a new thing, a way of restoring the relationship between himself and his people, as intended from Abraham onwards. He instituted a new covenant.

Reading: Jeremiah 31:31-34; Ezekiel 36:26-28
Key verse: Jeremiah 31:31

There is often great excitement in someone who has suddenly woken up to Jesus and the gospel. Usually even a glance at their eyes shows you a new sparkle. The Bible is a daily discovery for them and spiritual growth a thrilling experience. Some who have recently come to faith in our church are still exuberant a year or more on and they are infectious with the joy of Christ. They are a tonic to those of us who have been longer in the faith and it is great. The newness should never leave us whatever our circumstances; nor the excitement, wonder and joy. We should be the most joyful people on earth, even though much of the world thinks Christianity must be dull. So show the joy!

The foretelling of the New Covenant by Jeremiah (31:31 ff.), mentioned in the previous chapter, was a watershed moment in the history of God's people. It bridged the past with the future; the old with the new; failure and disobedience with the loving new relationship of love; the hopelessness with the new hope; the sacrificial system that faltered and lost its heart with the new way of forgiveness through the cross.

Although our Bible is split between the Old Testament/Covenant and the New Testament/Covenant the titles for the two sections might well have been BNC (Before the New Covenant) and INC (In the New Covenant). The whole New Testament is about God's covenant people even though the establishment of the covenant is not until the Last Supper.

Let us look in more detail at Jeremiah 31:31-34. It is emphatic that the New Covenant is not like the Old Moses Covenant. The end of verse 32 shows that the underlining failure of the Old Covenant was that although God loved them 'as a husband' they did not respond in love terms. They broke the covenant. There are shades of Hosea here. Hosea saw his own heartbreaking experience of his wife leaving him for prostitution and his allowing her to come back when her looks had withered and she was rejected by others, as preparing him to understand what Israel had done to God, as to a loving and faithful husband. God sees it all as a breaking of the covenant (Hos. 6:7; 8:1). Hosea believed that God would find a way to bring Israel back. The way in which this love could be restored in a new way, so that it could last, is at the core of the New Covenant.

● *Is loving faithfulness to God the outstanding mark of our Christian lives?*

When we come to verse 33 we see that the law is going to be written in their minds and on their hearts. Our Lord Jesus shows us that this will be the work which the Holy Spirit does in the new covenant relationship. For example: John 14:16,17: 'the Father . . . will give you another counsellor to be with you for ever – the Spirit of truth . . . *will be in you* (my italics), (v. 26): 'the Holy Spirit . . . will teach you all things', John 16:13,14: 'when . . . the Spirit of truth, comes, he will guide you into all truth . . . He will bring glory to me by taking from what is mine and making it known to you.' I have meditated on chapters 14 – 16 of John hundreds of times and though my understanding gets deeper there is still so much to draw from their amazing truths, especially over the indwelling of the Spirit.

How true it is that when we turned to Christ we began to 'see' spiritually. The Bible began to open up with freshness and power; sermons suddenly became more understandable and God's truth made wonderful sense of life and the world. This is true throughout our Christian life, isn't it? In my mid-seventies I can testify like millions of others that the Bible is still electric and God's truth constantly fresh and new. It is only possible because, as the New Covenant promise showed, the word has been written by the Holy Spirit into our minds and hearts.

Paul positively bubbles with this impact of the New Covenant. In 1 Corinthians 2:6-16 the waves of enthusiasm crash on to the beach foaming with wonder . . . the Spirit reveals God's wisdom to us but not to the world's wise, we have received the Spirit that we may understand what God has freely given us, we speak in words taught by the Spirit, explaining spiritual realities with Spirit-taught words. In 2 Corinthians 3:6 he shows how this is all part of the New Covenant: 'He (God) has made us . . . ministers of a new covenant – not of the letter but of the Spirit', and he sees his converts as (v. 3) 'a letter from Christ . . . written . . . with the Spirit of . . . God . . . on . . . human hearts.' Later in the chapter he speaks of the veil on the heart in the 'old covenant' (v. 14) and the way that in Christ the veil is lifted, the Spirit brings freedom and ongoing transformation can take place 'with ever-increasing glory'. It really is thrilling even just to write these words down, let alone to experience them.

- *Time to pause for a bit of personal bubbling! Why not share now in brief expressions of thanksgiving and praise; and express the desire for the Spirit to fill you freshly day by day?*
- *If in a group, share what the Spirit's indwelling has meant and does mean to you; perhaps in how the Bible opened up. You might have someone in the group like the man I knew who, after eventually coming to faith, said at the end of the service, 'The service was wonderful today . . . what's new?' 'You are, David!'*
- *If alone, think through all that the Spirit has done for you and in you since you came to Christ.*

Let us go back to Jeremiah 31 and see more about the new relationship in the last phrase of verse 33 and then in verse 34. 'I will be their God, and they will be my people.' He is, of course, referring to the New Covenant people. The New Testament knows that this is fulfilled with all in Christ, whether Jew or Gentile. Then the promise deepens. To a people used to all the intermediaries between them and God, with high priests and the holy of holies, the promise of direct personal fellowship with God, that all will know him from the least to the greatest, must have been almost too much to grasp. Do you not think that his hearers must have thought him a vague dreamer rather than a prophet of what God was indeed going to do?

In the New Testament and in our personal Christian life, we understand the wonderful truth that we can know God and relate to him. Jesus' words in John 15 about our abiding or remaining in him and he in us, or of our being branches in the vine, or of his love for us and of our need to respond in love are profoundly moving, even awesome. It is an awe Paul feels when he exclaims in 2 Corinthians 4:6 that it is the same God who created the world, and commanded light to come into it, who has shone into our hearts (one wants to pause and repeat it: our hearts, *our* hearts) and has given us 'the light of the knowledge of the glory of God in the face of Christ.'

I sat down for the lecture. In front of me sat a girl, obviously full of life and fun, and her hair bounced in front of me. I fell in love with the back of her head and the front was even better. We are now at our Golden Wedding Anniversary. We had great love for each other when we married and that has deepened across fifty years. A relationship has to grow. You learn new things about each other all the time; you learn to mould to each other and to share many things; you grow by serving or by going through illness or challenges in the work you share, and the relationship deepens. So it is with Christ, isn't it? You may be deeply in love with him in the early years of coming to him and then the relationship should grow and deepen and mature through the many experiences of life ahead. His love to us will not falter. It is our part and privilege to deepen our love for him.

While spending some months on the letter to the Philippians in preparation for giving the Bible Studies at a Keswick Convention a few years ago, I was blown apart by Philippians 3:10. It hit my heart with one mighty thump. I have not recovered. Every time I think about it, the effect is similar. 'I want to know Christ – yes, to know the power of his resurrection and the participation in his sufferings.' This was not written by a new Christian. This was written by the deepest theologian of his day, a man with a brilliant grasp of God's truth, a person with a track record of sacrificial service for Christ second to none, a man of mature years, not a youngster, and yet he still had this passion to know Christ more. I was winded and challenged. I thought of the 93-year-old clergyman in Australia who clasped my hand with tears streaming down his cheeks as he said: 'Thank you, thank you, for what you have taught me about Jesus tonight.' At ninety-three? What a humbling, moving and ever-memorable moment for me to meet such a man. I pray I might be like that if ever I reach the age of ninety-three.

- *We have pondered our relationship with Christ earlier in this book but let us do so again as we ask ourselves: 'How far has my relationship with Christ grown in the last twelve months?'*
- *If it hasn't, why not? Can you diagnose the causes?*
- *If it has, can you deepen it even more, as Paul longed to do? How?*

There is one other highly important part of the New Covenant prophecy in Jeremiah 31:34: 'For I will forgive their wickedness and will remember their sins no more.'

Those who heard this prophecy declaration could hardly have had the slightest inkling of what this was going to involve in the coming of Christ and his death for the sins of the whole world on the cross. As we shall recall later on in this book, that really would be new and would be called by Jesus the New Covenant in his blood.

Before we close this chapter, come fly with me. Let us do a flyover of the newness of the gospel. You may want to look at the passages slowly later on but, for the moment, ignore the references, just sit back, look at and revel in the newness that is ours in Christ. As we climb up from Jeremiah we may be reminded of other new promises in Isaiah 43:18,19; 65:17, or in Ezekiel 11:19; 36:26 – God doing a new thing, the vision of new heavens and earth. Now as we cross the border into the New Testament we see the crowds round Jesus and their amazement at his new teaching (Mk.1:27), we hear him teaching that the new wine of the gospel has to be in new wineskins (Mk. 2:21), we see Jesus giving the twelve a new commandment (Jn. 13:34). We move on over Paul's ministry journeys and we hear of the existence of new life in the Spirit (Rom. 6:4; 7:6) or of those in Christ being a new creation (2 Cor. 5:17; Gal. 6:15). In Ephesians 2:15 we hear of the uniting of Jew and Gentile in a 'new man'. Our holiness of living is then encouraged as we hear the charge to 'put on the new self' (Eph. 4:24) and we are encouraged by the fact of our ongoing renewal in 2 Corinthians 4:16 even when we are aged and decaying. As we rise higher, our eyes are lifted to the new heaven and new earth of 2 Peter 3:13 and Revelation 21. In Revelation we have a new name (2:17; 3:12) a new Jerusalem (3:12; 21:2) and as the flight ends we hear a new song (5:9; 14:3) which began when we were found in Christ and should have been fresh all the way until we are home and singing it with the vast gathering of the redeemed family of God. Has your heart taken a fillip? There is no doubt that in the New Covenant there is a multiple newness and we ourselves are renewed people through the grace, love and indwelling of our triune God. The New Covenant is new, new, wonderfully *new*!

● *What can you think of that you would like to add to the 'new' list, not from the Bible, but from your being in Christ?*

● *Why not sing a hymn of praise?*

FURTHER STUDY

You might like to work through the 'new' passages quoted in the final section of this chapter. It is rewarding to read them in context and to fill out the picture as they will then impact our lives and not just lift our spirits.

REFLECTION AND RESPONSE

Go back to 2 Corinthians 3 and see more fully what it says about the contrast between the old and new covenants. The blindness still exists today in all who have not turned to Christ. What do you think deepens the blindness of neighbours and friends outside Christ? Reflect on your prayer life and its regular detailed petitioning for these neighbours and friends by name. What do you actually pray for them? Does the praying need strengthening or freshening? Pray for them now.

CHAPTER 10

The institution of the New Covenant

Aim: To see the very heart of the New Covenant through Christ

FOCUS ON THE THEME:
The development of the covenant through the Old Testament, beginning with Abraham, has involved the love of God towards his people; it has been given by grace (undeserved by its recipients); it has involved sacrifice, often with blood; it has called for a commitment to follow the Lord, to walk in his ways and to obey his will, often being sealed by the sprinkling of blood.

All this is now here in the New Testament (Covenant). It is all because God so loved the world (Jn. 3:16). Grace and truth came by Jesus Christ (Jn. 1:17). The New Testament not only moves towards the cross, to the supreme sacrifice for our sins and to the shed blood, it also dynamites our way of thinking and living, from the Sermon on the Mount and on through the apostolic letters. As we look at the New Covenant we look first at its establishment with our Saviour's sacrifice and shed blood.

Reading: Luke 22:7-20; Hebrews 9:11-15
Key verse: Luke 22:20

The boy sat on a block of hay. All around him was the beauty of the Peak District. He had never seen anything like it before. A few days before, he had heard a group of people singing in his inner-city street. He had come out of his garret room in the attic and gone down into the street. He heard someone speaking in between the singing. When they moved to the next street, he followed; and then to the next street. I noticed him following and listening. At the end I went over to him. His mother was dead; his father was an alcoholic. His conditions of living, in a garret room, were awful. He was aged sixteen and worked in a tannery; his schooling had been a failure. The young people of the church were going off to camp in the Peak District for the weekend. Would he like to come? Would he not! The cost was covered for him. He came. Now on the Sunday morning he was sitting there on this bale of hay, in the sunshine and with the hills of the Peak District around him. I spoke about the Old Testament sacrifices and explained in simple words and action the truth of Leviticus 1:3: 'If the offering is a burnt offering from the herd, you are to offer a male without defect. You are to lay your hand on the head of the burnt offering, and it will be accepted on your behalf to make atonement for you.'

I saw the scales drop off the lad's eyes. Although he had never seen a bull or a sheep nor had he ever been to a church or heard the gospel, except in the street services a few nights before, he totally grasped the truth. He laid his hand on Christ as the one who died for him. His life rapidly changed. He was welcomed into a Christian home as one of the family. He went on to qualify in mental nursing and then as a State Registered Nurse, eventually going on to lecturing on nursing. Becoming a Christian was a total transformation.

When the lad put his hand on Christ he was accepting the New Covenant of eternal salvation, made possible by the once and for all sacrifice and shed blood of his Saviour. He has renewed that covenant trust thousands of times since, particularly when putting out his hand to receive the bread and the wine at Holy Communion. For this, of course, is how the New Covenant was established.

- *If you are in a group, did anyone present wake up to the truth by a similar awakening to the meaning of Christ's atoning sacrifice?*
- *How much do you value the way in which Christ's final sacrifice for sins was prepared for in the Old Testament?*

Look at Luke 22:20: 'he took the cup, saying, "This cup is the new covenant in my blood, which is poured out for you."' Now look on to 1 Corinthians 11:25: 'after supper he took the cup, saying, "This cup is the new covenant in my blood; do this, whenever you drink it, in remembrance of me."' In both, our Lord refers to the making of the New Covenant.

However, we note that in Matthew's account of the Last Supper (Mt. 26:28) the words are 'This is my blood of the covenant which is poured out for many for the forgiveness of sins.' Mark 14:24 is the same, except that it does not have 'for the forgiveness of sins'. The word 'new' is not used in either but a footnote under both in NIV and other versions tells us that some manuscripts say 'new'. There is really no significance about the omission of 'new' as our Lord is obviously referring to the New Covenant. Luke would have carefully researched his writing, with his doctor's accuracy, as would Paul. There is no other mention of covenant in the Gospels before this, except in Zecharaiah's song (Lk. 1:72). The decks are cleared for the establishing of the New Covenant.

Now we need to use our zoom facility to look more closely at what happened in the Upper Room. Notice that 'covenant' is only used of the wine, not of the bread. This fact can come as quite a surprise. In Matthew and Mark, Jesus takes the bread, breaks it and says 'Take and eat; this is my body.' Luke adds 'given for you'. Paul, in 1 Corinthians 11, adds instead 'which is for you'. Both Luke and Paul then add 'in remembrance of me'. The covenant is not mentioned. All versions have 'this is my body' but with the wine, the words are not just 'This is my blood' but 'This is my blood of the covenant' or 'This is the new covenant in my blood'. Why is this?

We need to go back to Exodus 24:5-8 to help us understand. Here there is first a sacrifice of burnt offerings and fellowship offerings. The blood is then sprinkled on the altar. The Book of the Covenant is then read to the people and they promise to do everything the Lord has said. Only after that response is the blood sprinkled on the people and Moses says, 'This is the blood of the covenant that the LORD has made with you in accordance with all these words.' The blood that is sprinkled comes from the sacrifice. The words are those later used by our Lord at the Last Supper. We must see a link and a deeper meaning.

The sacrifice of Christ on the cross is once and for all and we stand on this with assurance of faith. In Exodus the blood sprinkled on to the people is a direct identifying of the people with the sacrifice, like laying hands on it. They make it their own. The blood also seems to be linked to their response of obeying the Lord and walking in his ways as it is not sprinkled on the people until they have made that response. It seals them in their covenant relationship and responsibility.

How far can we press this for ourselves as New Covenant believers? In Matthew 26:28 we have a linking of the blood to forgiveness, added to the words, 'This is my blood of the covenant.' In 1 John 1:7 we are told that if we walk in the light, as he is in the light, we have fellowship with one another, and 'the blood of Jesus, his Son, purifies us from all sin.' The two aspects of the blood as the mark of redemption and yet also as a mark of holy living go on through the New Testament. We are 'justified by his blood', 'have redemption through his blood' (Rom. 5:9; Eph.1:7) and so on. Peter gives us the double aspect in 1 Peter 1: 'for obedience to Jesus Christ and sprinkling by his blood' (v. 2) and then 'you were redeemed . . . with the precious blood of Christ, a lamb without blemish or defect' (vv.18,19).

So now let us come back to the Holy Communion service. We take the bread and hear 'this is my body given for you' and we should, I suggest, be offering praise and thanks for that once and for all sacrifice of our Saviour in which we have trusted and by which we are saved. As we put the bread in our mouths it will be an identifying with that sacrifice, like laying hands on it, with a quiet joy of assurance of being his people by grace. Then we take the cup. Now the covenant word comes into action. As we drink the wine we are taking the cup of the New Covenant in his blood. We are assured by it of forgiveness of our sins, of cleansing through the sacrifice of the cross and of an on-going cleansing as we keep on confessing our sins and walking in the light. Yet we are also re-pledging ourselves to the New Covenant, to walk a holy life, sprinkled with the blood of the covenant, wanting to walk in his ways and according to his word. The fresh awakening to this aspect has made a big difference to my own reception of the bread and wine. All this is to be taken seriously and will need more moments with God than are usually possible at the time of reception.

In the Prayer Book Communion service the invitation to partake is to all who 'truly and earnestly repent' of their sins and 'are in love and charity' with their neighbours and who 'intend to lead a new life, following the commandments of God, and walking . . . in his holy ways.' The double aspect is very clear.

● *Think through the meanings of receiving the bread and then of receiving the wine.*

The seriousness of the Lord's Supper and the New Covenant at its institution is underlined in 1 Corinthians 11:18-29. They were far from being in love and charity with their neighbour. They thought more of themselves than of others. In verses 27-29 Paul severely warns about the careless attitude of some there who eat and drink of the cup unworthily and so sin against the body and blood of the Lord. They are to examine themselves before participating, for those who eat and drink without discerning the body of Christ 'eat and drink judgment on themselves.' These are very strong words; a very strong warning. Not heeding it, says Paul, has made them weak and ill in their Christian lives, even falling asleep. So why is Holy Communion such a quick, added-on, get-through-quickly part of worship in some churches? And why is confession not taken seriously? Does such carelessness not also cause spiritual weakness? How much is taught and preached about Holy Communion? Yes, it is done in some churches and the service is reverent, real and carefully prepared. So are those participating. Yet I have sometimes been deeply saddened by the carelessness of a Communion service.

● *Does this ring bells for you? What can you do about it, if so?*
● *The 1662 Church of England Prayer Book contains three exhortations, which can be found in the middle of the Holy Communion Service. One is giving notice of a coming*

celebration of Holy Communion; one a warning to those who do not bother to come; the third at the time of the service itself. They are worth reading if you can lay your hands on a Prayer Book but here now are parts of the first one, showing the seriousness with which the Reformers regarded the service. Please read it aloud.

● *The minister describes the sacrament of Communion as 'so divine and comfortable a thing to them who receive it worthily, and so dangerous to them that will presume to receive it unworthily; my duty is to exhort you in the mean season to consider the dignity of that holy mystery, and the great peril of the unworthy receiving thereof; and so to search and examine your own consciences, (and that not lightly, and after the manner of dissemblers with God; but so) that you may come clean and holy to such a heavenly feast in the marriage-garment required by God in holy Scripture, and be received as worthy partakers of that holy Table.'*

● *What does Holy Communion mean to you?*

● *Do an honest self-appraisal about how you approach a Holy Communion service.*

Before we end this chapter, we must turn to Hebrews, for here what we have been looking at is fully expounded. It is written to Jewish believers who were on the 'wobble' in their faith because of the lingering hold that outward ceremonies had on them. It argues strongly that Jesus is the Son of God who lives for ever and no one else comes near him, not even Moses. He shows them that what Christ did was to bring about the final once-for-all sacrifice for the sins of the world, that he was the final High Priest and that he was the sacrifice offered.

The covenant is referred to more than twenty times. The writer has a grip on covenant theology. In 7:22 Jesus is 'the guarantee of a better covenant' because he was a priest for ever after the order or Melchizedek who preceded Abraham. The New Covenant is superior to the old because it is founded on better promises (8:6) and by calling this covenant new he has made the old one 'obsolete' (8:13). He is the mediator of a New Covenant because he obtained eternal redemption by his own blood, entering the Most Holy place by his blood once and for all (9:12-15). There is also the cleansing by the blood of Christ in verse 14 'so that we may serve the living God!' It is also in Hebrews (10:10-18) that the New Covenant prophecy of Jeremiah 31:34 is seen as fulfilled and the words of Jeremiah that 'Their sins and lawless acts I will remember no more' are quoted and then followed with: 'And where these have been forgiven, there is no longer any sacrifice for sin.'

The New Covenant is final, complete, totally adequate and eternal. Because of it (Heb.10:19-25) we have confidence to enter the Most Holy Place by the blood of Jesus. We also have responsibilities to live as covenant people with faith, sprinkled hearts, hope, love, good deeds and meeting together. Living as Christ's covenant people is thrilling, challenging, fulfilling and sometimes demanding, as we shall consider together in the next chapters.

FURTHER STUDY

It is very helpful and revealing to study the use of 'blood' in the Bible. You might like to look at this selection of New Testament references: Romans 5:9; 1 Corinthians 10:16 (where Paul shows that Communion is not just remembrance but participation – something worth thinking about and discussing); Ephesians 1:7; 2:13; Colossians 1:20; 1 Peter 1:2; 1:19; 1 John.1:7; 5:6. We have not looked at Revelation, so see 1:5; 5:9; 7:14; 12:11; 19:13.

REFLECTION AND RESPONSE

There is seriousness in the institution of the New Covenant as at its centre stands the Lamb of God, the one who gave himself as the final sacrifice for the sins of the world, who shed his blood for us. There is also seriousness in our being covenant people marked with the blood of Christ, rather like the door of the Passover room was in the exodus from Egypt. In Hebrews 10:29 it speaks in the strongest terms of any who have 'trampled the Son of God under foot, who have treated as an unholy thing the blood of the covenant that sanctified them, and who have insulted the Spirit of grace'. So let us reflect on how deeply we are his covenant people, both in our faith-relationship to Christ and our daily cleansing, as well as in the way we live in holiness.

• Reflect again on your attitude to Holy Communion.

• You will no doubt wish to respond to your Lord as seems appropriate for you; you may also want to offer prayer for those who are moving or have moved to trampling under foot the Son of God and the blood of the covenant that they may turn back before it is too late and become again true covenant people.

CHAPTER 11

Jesus shows us how to live by grace

Aim: To see how our Lord expects us to challenge legalism by grace, as we observe him doing that in his life

---

FOCUS ON THE THEME:
When we turn to the New Testament we are, of course, turning to the New Covenant. Although the institution of the New Covenant was in the broken body and shed blood of our Lord Jesus, the whole testament is concerned with becoming and living as New Covenant people. In this chapter we see how our Lord challenged the accepted legalistic view at almost every point and so disturbed the religious leaders that they were determined to destroy him. The cross was the outcome and although it was the climax of the clash between grace and law, it showed starkly the failure of law and the triumph of grace.

Reading: John 1:9-18
Key verse: John 1:17

The man had not been to Europe before. He hired a car and as he approached a roundabout (at a speed just over the limit) he saw a flash of light. So puzzled was he by this that he went round and back at a faster speed to see what was happening. The light flashed again. By now he thought someone was trying to attract his attention or was just being a nuisance so he sped round again. The light flashed on the speed camera for the third time. The police fined him heavily for all three incidents and almost took away his driving licence. Here was law without grace. Grace would have seen it was all unintentional and that the man was fazed by the strange experience (he presumably came from a country without such cameras). A token fine (if any) and a good laugh would have been grace's response. The law had no mercy.

It is this atmosphere into which the Son of God enters. In spite of the New Covenant prophecy, legalism still reigned in religion. So, when Jesus came 'full of grace and truth', the clash began. It was not just his teaching. It was supremely himself, his person, his actions, his love and his humility. In Mark 1:41 he reaches out and touches the leper. That action, unthinkable to most people of the day, was sheer grace and love. Then in Mark 2:1,12, when he is surrounded by a huge crowd in Capernaum, possibly at Peter's house, and he preaches the word to them, he also shows his divine authority. The men, desperate to get their sick friend to Jesus, rip off part of the roof and lower the man to Jesus' feet. It was when Jesus said to the man 'Your sins are forgiven' that the teachers of the law were infuriated but, when Jesus proved his authority by healing the man, everyone was 'amazed.' Legalism was overcome by the outflow of grace. The clash was beginning.

The security protector on my computer tells me quite frequently that it has repelled an attack. Hopefully none of the attackers will get through. Jesus faced endless attacks from the law thinkers. He repelled them with grace and truth, time after time after time. Soon after the Capernaum clash the Pharisees attack again (Mk. 2:15-17), this time because he eats with tax collectors and sinners. Law would not allow such defilement. Grace does it because, says Jesus, these people are like those who are ill and they need a physician. Immediately they attack again (Mk. 2:18-22), this time because the disciples of Jesus are not fasting like those of John the Baptist. Jesus replies that no one fasts when the bridegroom is with them but only when he has gone, and then he goes on to speak of the uselessness of pouring new wine into old wineskins and that new wine has to go into new wineskins. The New Covenant teaching will need New Covenant ways of expression in worship, in church structures and in holy living. As we take breath, we plunge straight on in Mark 2:23-27, to the Pharisees' challenge over the Sabbath. Here was very strict law, down to the minutiae of what you could not do (and a little on what you could do). The disciples had actually picked some ears of corn. What a sin. Jesus responds with a perfect counterpoint from the Old Testament, the time when David (and the Pharisees would not argue about David) went into the temple so that he and his hungry companions could eat the consecrated bread – a far greater 'sin' than a few ears of corn. The need was paramount. Grace acted to meet the need, not to meet the law. The *coup de grace* (literally) was then delivered in our Lord's memorable words that the Sabbath was made for man, not man for the Sabbath. And 'the Son of Man is Lord even of the Sabbath,' he adds. All this is in one chapter of Mark's Gospel, showing how Mark saw the clash of law and grace right from the beginning. The New Covenant was already being worked out 'on the ground' by its Lord.

● *Imagine yourself having been brought up with the Pharisees' teaching, having been drilled with the law and the huge number of interpretations and rules that had been added.*

● *How would you have felt, hearing and watching Jesus and then waking up to grace and its thrilling liberation, newness and joy?*

● *Did you grow up with legalism, perhaps in a strict church that infused more fear than love, more law than grace and which perhaps warned you off contact with other denominations? If so, think back (share, if in a group) what the liberation of grace has meant to you and how far legalism still keeps trying to raise its head.*

Our son Andrew and his wife Rachel went to church, as usual, while on holiday in Norfolk. The two elderly ladies behind them said in loud voices: 'How disgraceful coming to church in jeans!' Andrew wanted to turn round and say, 'And I am the son of a Bishop, too!' In the church where he is now vicar, a new convert and two of his contacts usually keep their woollen hats or caps on through the service. Law would condemn and tell them to remove them. Grace sees their souls as more important and just smiles. Grace operates in that church.

When one of our much-loved nieces was diagnosed with lymphoblastic leukaemia, someone at the church door said to me, 'Until you lay hands on her, she will not recover.' Another said, 'Until you anoint her with oil, she will not recover.' Sheer legalism! I replied to both that although both symbols were helpful to the sick person and I often used them, it was not the symbol that healed but God.

When I took a bunch of tough young people, in their later teens, away for a weekend early in my ministry, I was still very sabbatarian and forbade all games on the Sunday. The inevitable result was that they wandered off and came back late, drunk. Then, some months later, I was helped to see that although the Sabbath looks back to the resting of the seventh day of creation, the Lord's Day looks forward to eternal rest, to heaven and glory. It is a day of joyful worship and service and is to be infused with the grace and joy of the New Covenant.

When I was first ordained in 1956 there was almost no youth music for churches. Yet a new wave of rock and roll had begun in the secular music world with Bill Haley and the Comets in 1955. The endeavours to meet the challenge resulted not only in *Youth Praise*, which swept through the nation's youth groups, but also in getting young Christians to learn and use the guitar for worship. It was bitterly opposed by some. We heard of organists walking out. There were those who spoke (usually in a loud voice) of the devil having been allowed into the church. Choirs with a legalistic attitude to what constituted church music opposed the guitar group in their church. Grace acted differently. Then the good musicians helped the young people to get off the three-chord trick and to become better musicians. I remember one robed choir reaching down for their guitars to play during the Communion administration. In some churches the war is still on, though now it is often the other way round, with wonderful older hymns banished in favour of songs and guitars alone. There are also those who will not go to worship unless the Bible is read in the Elizabethan language of King James' version and the service is from the 1662 prayer book. There are those who readily accept the revised language of newer Bible versions but react against any attempt to do the same with hymns. Grace is far bigger than all that.

● *What examples of legalism in the church, past and present, come to your mind?*

● *If they are current legalisms, how can you challenge them by grace? E.g. if it is expected that everyone wears best clothes for church, would you be prepared to wear casual clothes if it helped outsiders to feel more at home? The opposite also applies in some churches.*

● *More difficult to challenge but necessary to do so are those churches that seem to think most other Christians are in error and that they alone are right; or where there is heavy 'shepherding' which has become control over people's lives; or when it is demanded that you accept the church's interpretation on all aspects of its teaching or you are not saved. Is it best to leave and pray for them or stay and try to change the situation?*

Let us walk further into the Gospels with our Lord. In Matthew 9:10-13, there is the account of the Pharisees criticising Jesus for eating with tax collectors and sinners, as he sits at dinner in Matthew's house. Our Lord refers them back to Hosea 6:6, 'I desire mercy (covenant love), not sacrifice'. Hosea's words had been part of the exposure of the Old Covenant. He had used the powerful example of his wife's unfaithfulness to show just what Israel had done to God. They had lost all love for God and their worship had become a legalistic sham. His words about God desiring covenant love prepared the way for the New Covenant and Jesus now claims them within the coming of the New Covenant.

In Matthew 15:2-20 the Pharisees come in to battle again: 'Why do your disciples break the traditions of the elders? They don't wash their hands before they eat!' Before Jesus exposes this criticism directly, he uses the illustration of how 'by their tradition' they get round the commandment to honour father and mother. They thereby 'nullify the word of God' (v. 6). Tradition does that so often and I have sometimes seen sickening evidences of this in churches. However, Jesus then again pushes the issue back to New Covenant prophecy in the Old Testament. He quotes Isaiah about people honouring with lips but their heart being far from him, the very issue that caused the collapse of Jerusalem and the Exile, and which resulted in Jeremiah's New Covenant prophecy.

There is still more in grace's counter-exposure of legalism. What does really defile? Unwashed hands or unwashed hearts? It is hearts that produce (v. 19) 'evil thoughts, murder, adultery, sexual immorality, theft, false testimony, slander.' The basic law given at Sinai with grace and love is upheld but legalism is trounced.

Jesus did not cancel God's true law of love. When he is challenged about divorce (Mt.19:3-10) he goes back to Genesis and says that Moses' allowance on this was because their 'hearts were hard'. Grace was meeting hardness, as it still has to do on this issue today. In Matthew 22:15-22 the Pharisees try to 'trap him' on the matter of the poll tax but our Lord's reply leaves them defeated, yet again, as he says, 'Give to Caesar what is Caesar's, and to God what is God's.' It is appropriate for us to recall again John 7:13 – 8:11, where the incident of the woman taken in adultery is a powerful clash of law and grace. Law condemns and wants to stone the woman to death. Our Lord challenges the condemners about their own sin, and then shows utter grace to the woman, even though he uses the word 'sin' of her actions as he tells her to sin no more. It is grace abounding.

The heart is the key to grace. The rich young man (Mt.19:16) was a careful keeper of the law but his heart was tied up with his possessions. So our Lord's response to his question, 'what good thing must I do to get eternal life?' was that he should sell all he had, give to the poor and start following Jesus. It was devastating. Yet in this man's case it was the only way for him to break the grip of materialism and to stop relying on legal observances for assurance. History has since included many who *have* acted radically over the hold of wealth and have found new life in Christ.

When a lawyer asks 'who is my neighbour?' Jesus' telling of the story of the Good Samaritan (Lk. 10:30 ff.) is a powerful exposition on legalism and grace. It was so clear and direct. The legalists walked by on the other side. The despised Samaritan acts with grace, love, cost and possible risk to his life. The story must have brought a huge resonance from the crowd and a devastating impact on the legalists.

The disciples themselves had to eradicate legalistic thinking from their minds. We see this with Peter in Matthew 18:21: 'Lord, how many times shall I forgive someone who sins against me? Up to seven times?' Jesus smashes such legalistic thinking by saying that Peter should forgive seventy-seven times. Grace does not calculate; nor does it stop at some point. The story that Jesus then tells, of the man owing a huge debt to the king and being forgiven, yet not having mercy on someone who owes him a small amount, puts it into a vivid perspective. The grace of forgiveness we have received in Christ is so great that our acts of forgiveness are puny in comparison and all who receive such abounding grace from Christ must show it by action in their attitudes to others or be exposed as hypocrites. It was not the only issue on which Peter needed to be sorted out but it is a powerful one for us to hear again and live out.

● *Pause to reflect on this section. Does it raise issues in your own life that need attention, such as forgiveness of others who have hurt you or quick judgemental attitudes or a materialistic bias?*

Les Miserables is a story in which grace is so powerfully demonstrated that the book and the musical are actually a powerful Christian testimony. If you know it well, bear with me in my recounting it here. When John Valjean escapes from prison and comes to the Bishop's house, he is met with utter grace. He is welcomed (though not by the

Bishop's housekeeper who has no grace, only judgement), he is invited to the dinner table and given a comfortable room for the night. His theft of the silver plates and cutlery during the night and quiet departure from the house was like throwing grace back in the Bishop's face. Yet when the police bring him back to the Bishop, triumphantly, they in turn meet grace head-on when the Bishop chides Valjean for not taking the candlesticks too, and orders his glowering housekeeper to go and get them. 'You gave him the silver?' ask the police, incredulously. 'Yes' says the Bishop. It is an amazing act of grace. The musical does not have time to go on where the book then goes. In the book, Valjean sees a boy playing with a coin. The boy drops the coin. Valjean puts his foot on it. The boy pleads to have his coin back. Valjean refuses. The boy goes off crying. It is then that Valjean is overcome with the realisation of what he has done. He weeps his heart out. He searches everywhere for the boy but does not find him. He then truly grasps the depths of the amazing grace that was extended to him and how deeply sinful is his own sinful lack of grace over a mere coin. It powerfully retells the story Jesus told in Matthew 18, although this time there is repentance. Yet, in the story, his pursuer, police-agent Inspector Javert, becomes more and more consumed with anger, with an all-consuming passion to put Valjean back behind bars and with vengeance filling his heart. When he eventually meets up with Valjean at the revolution barricade he finds himself in Valjean's power. Valjean presses the gun to Javert's head and then, with utter grace, tells him to go. The contrast between his embittered heart and Valjean's grace is too much. He commits suicide. Hatred destroyed; grace triumphed. New Covenant living is all about grace.

FURTHER STUDY

Go back over all or some of the Bible passages mentioned in this chapter and read them with care, thought and prayer.

REFLECTION AND RESPONSE

The whole chapter raises so many points on grace and, where any have 'struck home' for us, now may be the time to reflect and respond in a time with our Lord.

CHAPTER 12

Radical New Covenant teaching: the Sermon on the Mount

Aim: To look at the Sermon on the Mount in the light of the relationship between grace and law and to see how grace gets to the heart of an issue

FOCUS ON THE THEME:
John Stott called his wonderful exposition of the Sermon on the Mount *Christian Counter-culture*. It is a superb title, for its gets to the root of Jesus' teaching. Attitudes are challenged and radical transformation is expected; laws are broken open to expose their narrowness and to give them a motivation of love; legalism is exposed; grace and love reign supreme. To some it sets an impossible standard; to New Covenant believers it is a thrilling liberation from legalism into grace.

Reading: Matthew 5:17-20 and 5:44-45
Key verses: Matthew 5:17; 5:44

The telephone rang on a Sunday afternoon. 'Michael, I think I have the answer. Margaret and I will come up to the evening service to show you.' It was Robert Potter, our superb architect. He had wrestled with the plans for adapting the interior of All Souls, Langham Place, resulting from the plan to build a hall underneath. Eventually he had pondered the mind and intention of John Nash, the original architect, and now had plans that took hold of those principles and adapted the church accordingly, though meeting its modern requirements. Then there was another call. It was the church archivist. 'I have discovered a copy of Nash's original plan and will show it to you this evening.' It seemed far more than a coincidence. Later that day we laid both plans out alongside each other and saw how right the new plans were. We were on track. By removing Victorian additions that had marred the original plan; by putting back Nash's choir gallery, re-raking the galleries for everyone to be able to see the preacher, having the pulpit moveable to the centre and so on, the church would be expressing Nash's original intentions, yet with a fresh and fuller development of those intentions.

That is exactly what is happening in the Sermon on the Mount (Mt. 5 – 7). Christ takes us back to the Creator's original plan and intention. Here is a dramatic exposure of the false or inadequate interpretations of the commandments that have been added and a fresh and fuller development of the commandments, as God had intended. The Author is speaking. He is showing the fulfilment of law in love. This is the guide for his New Covenant people.

However, at first we are stopped in our tracks when we read (5:17): 'Do not think that I have come to abolish the Law and the Prophets: I have come not to abolish them but to fulfil them.' To those who want to ignore the Old Testament and be just New Testament Christians these are uncomfortable words. Back in the second century AD, Marcion thought them more than uncomfortable. He could not accept them so he rewrote them: 'I have come to abolish . . .' His heretical teaching was popular and many of his churches became established all over the Roman Empire, lasting for more than two hundred years. Marcion was wrong and he stripped his followers of their godly heritage, beginning with Abraham. We believe that the New Covenant is a huge leap forward from the Old but it is also the fulfilling of the Old.

In our day we have seen the so-called 'new morality' which basically puts love as the sole guide and relegates or even eliminates law. It seems attractive as there is no doubt that love is the key to the whole Bible. When one of its popular exponents said, for instance, that if a mature woman knew of a young man having problems about sex she could take him and teach him, not by words but action, he claimed that this was love (no concept of sin) and that where there was love there was God. This has become the gospel for many, rather than the gospel of sins forgiven through the cross, and has little room for the law or the rest of God's word. This is also why, when people on both sides of the homosexuality debate speak of the gospel, they may be talking about different gospels, some seeing the gospel as only love without rules and with the cross just as an example of love; others seeing the gospel as love fulfilling God's law and the cross as where love and justice met.

Jesus says (5:17) that he has come not to abolish the law and the prophets 'but to fulfil them.' Just as at Langham Place, the original architect's intentions had been spoilt by a lot of additions and alterations, so God's Ten Commandments had been overlaid by thousands of additions and detailed rules. In both cases the clearing of the additions enabled the original intentions to be fulfilled. C.S. Lewis, commenting on Psalm 19, said he found it understandable that there needed to be statutes but he was puzzled that the psalmist could speak of them as 'sweeter than honey' (v. 10).Then, as he studied the psalm more, he realised that the beauty and sweet reasonableness of the law is increasingly evident when seen in contrast to the paganism that surrounds us. For me, it seems like a well-tuned engine, running as the manufacturer intended. In the perfect fulfilling of the instructions, there is a quiet steady hum to the engine. We even say an engine sounds 'sweet'. The manufacturer's instructions are for the very best. So are the instructions of the God of love. The law is fulfilled as he intended when lived by love.

That love undergirds and interprets law is seen by our Lord's answer to the Pharisees in Matthew 22:34-40. They ask: 'Teacher, which is the greatest commandment in the Law?' Their attempt to trap him into a detailed response was turned back on their own heads with the answer that loving God with all one's heart, soul and mind, and loving one's neighbour as oneself were the two greatest commandments and then he added: 'All the Law and the Prophets hang on these two commandments.' Thus, these two did not push the other commandments into a siding but were the motivations and overriding interpretation of them all. This helps us to understand 5:18: 'until heaven and earth disappear, not the smallest letter, not the least stroke of a pen (I did like the old KJV with 'jot' and 'tittle'!) will by any means disappear from the Law until everything is accomplished.' Love may fulfil the law but it does not trample on law. Love cannot eliminate honouring parents, or allow stealing or murder or adultery. Nor does it try to take broad principles and relegate detail. It clears the human additions and gets back to motive. Only by this can New Covenant people have a righteousness that 'surpasses that of the Pharisees'. The Pharisees tried to keep the law; we are to have the love that sees law as Jesus did.

What Jesus teaches in the Sermon on the Mount and beyond is what he means by the fulfilling of the law and, although the law will cease when earth and heaven cease, our Lord's words 'will never pass away' (Mt. 24:35). So, as New Covenant people, we hang upon his Word.

● *Turn to Romans 13:8-10 and see how Paul handles the same theme as he shows that loving one's neighbour does not take away the detail of the Ten Commandments but fulfils them. He has this penetrating phrase: 'Let no debt remain outstanding, except the continuing debt to love one another'.*

● *How far is your keeping of the Ten Commandments, and the keeping of our Lord's commands and teaching, a matter of law or a desire to live with moral beauty fulfilled by love and inspired by the love of your Saviour?*

● *What does it mean to you that we are to love our neighbour as ourselves (James 2:8 calls it the 'royal law')? It could be helpful to think of how we love ourselves and then think about how we love our neighbour. For instance, if we make a mistake, do we hope to be forgiven; now apply that to your neighbour making a mistake . . . and so on.*

The key words in chapter 5 are 'But I tell you' (vv. 22,28,32,34,39,44). We sit up and listen. It is the Author speaking. It is like feeling the waters under the keel as your boat begins to sail. We feel afloat on a new wave of teaching that liberates, inspires, explains and interprets. This is linking back to Abraham and Moses but is now first-hand opening up of what God intended all along. Do we not want to keep saying 'Yes!', 'Yes!', 'Yes!'? It is so refreshing and radical; it makes such sense; it calls us to a standard of living, as New Covenant people, that well and truly exceeds that of the scribes and Pharisees. I have never forgotten the time in my first curacy when I had to deal with a boy who stole the wallet of a fellow-leader. I called at his home and spoke with him and his parents. In the course of events that followed I heard his mother say of me one day, 'If only he had shown some love.' It was a fair rebuke and it went through me like a sword. Yes, the law had to operate but love needed to be dominant. I had not begun in the school of the Sermon on the Mount. I needed to grow in New Covenant living.

In 5:21-26 there is no cancellation of the law about murder but the fulfilling of it goes further than anyone had envisaged in the Old Covenant. It is to be widened to anger, says the author, and the footnote says that some versions add 'without a cause'. 'Raca' is an attitude of utter contempt, regarding someone as stupid. 'Fool' is showing contempt for someone's character, calling someone a rogue. 'Love your neighbour as yourself' sounds in our ears, but if, as seems likely, 'brother and sister' refers to fellow-Christians, then we are pitched into the church and the later command to love one another. It all makes sense. It is fulfilling the law by love.

Adultery is the next commandment which our Lord opens up (5:27-30). The Pharisees tried to confine this to the act itself but Jesus blows it open to include lust. We have been onlookers to what happened between President Bill Clinton and Monica Lewinsky, where there was a similar endeavour to adjust the meaning of adultery. In Jesus' eyes the intention of the heart is what really matters and that is what really hurt Clinton's family. Our Lord expects strong self-control, not to be legalistic but to keep to true love in a marriage relationship. This seems totally ignored by those who now do not regard adultery as a sin. Way back in Job we read (31:1-7) of Job making a covenant that with his eyes he would not look lustfully at a virgin. He also says he would be guilty 'if my heart has been led by my eyes'. Job knew it was an issue of the heart and of self-control as a follower of God. Thankfully, those of us in the New Covenant, seeking to follow Christ's words, have the Holy Spirit within us, to help us live as Jesus intends.

● *Is repentance needed for failing over the issues raised in this chapter so far?*
● *Do you see Christ's standards as restrictive or 'sweeter than honey'? If the latter, spend a moment praising and thanking, and then re-expressing your love for him and your desire to be better at loving your neighbour.*

An 'eye for eye, and tooth for tooth' (5:38-42) was not in the Ten Commandments, of course, but was originally trying to be a restraint on the exacting of punishment far exceeding the crime. That could only be temporary. Christ does not now approve it, or expand it. This is practical ruling but not divine law, so he demolishes it. We hear it quoted frequently today, not least in the Middle East. Christ blew it apart two thousand years ago. Recently I have been to a lecture by an eminent Jewish medical professor on the theme of 'playing God'. It was fascinating and professional but at almost every point I wanted to get up on my feet and say, 'But Christ'. Although I agreed with most of what he said, it did not go far enough. It stopped in the Old Testament. Almost every point would have sprung into God's fuller perspective with an understanding of the New Testament. Similarly, when I hear 'an eye for an eye and a tooth for a tooth' I want to stand on my feet and say, 'But Christ' (usually it is only my wife Myrtle and the radio or television set that would hear!).

Suddenly we are in New Covenant living. Turn the cheek, give the shirt, go the extra mile, give to those who want to borrow (though this is unlikely to have included obvious cheats). This is a quantum leap. It is expressing love in very practical terms. The slap on the cheek would probably have been a deliberate insult, as it was to Jesus at his trial; it is thought that the shirt may have been demanded by an enemy; the extra mile might have been when pressed to do so by the army, as with Simon of Cyrene on the road to the cross. Thus all circumstances could have called for revenge; all could be seen as a deep sense of injustice done. This rings bells with me as I think back over my life and incidents in earlier years where I felt deeply angered by what seemed to be injustice. Christ commands us to overcome it with stunning action to prevent revenge; self-giving love is required.

The point is reinforced in 5:43-48. Christ first dismantles a misquote. 'Love your neighbour' is there in Leviticus 19:18, in the context of not seeking revenge, but not 'hate your enemy'. It is always good to check Scripture quotes. A broadcast preacher used verse 43 as a text a few months ago. I could not believe it. One day a self-opinionated man who 'did good deeds' (collecting money from some and giving it with a flourish to others) told me he had been on holiday and had experienced sun all the time. He was not being funny when he added, 'That's what the Bible says, doesn't it, Rector, the sun shines on the righteous.' I was temporarily speechless until I remembered the accurate text (here in 5:45): 'He causes his sun to rise on the evil and the good, and sends rain on the righteous and the unrighteous.' Of course, it is there to teach us that we too must love our enemies rather than hate them. We are to pray for those who persecute us. It is a fulfilling of the law in a glorious liberation, a fresh wind that goes on sweeping through New Covenant teaching.

At Dr Martin Luther King's funeral this moving statement was made: 'This man had no bitterness in his heart, no rancour in his soul and no revenge in his mind.'

New Covenant living has the aim of being 'perfect' like our heavenly Father (5:48), with a love that goes well beyond what is respectable or socially the norm. Love is the motivation; the heart; the context. It is love fulfilling the law, and proving it to be 'sweeter than honey'.

● *How do you get on about injustices done to you? Are you able to deal with the natural feelings of wanting revenge? Or is this an area for seeking fresh help from the Holy Spirit?*

● *Is there anyone you feel you can never forgive? You must. Swallow pride; look at Christ's love; act.*

● *Paul in Romans 12:21 speaks of overcoming evil with good and he uses the example of feeding one's enemy. Has this been possible in your life? Have you seen it in others?*

● *Do you see its relevance in the world of today, especially in conflict zones between nations or people or in families?*

FURTHER STUDY

Study chapters 5 – 7 of Matthew over a period of days.

For fuller study, get a copy of John Stott's *Christ the Controversialist*.[6] It is a masterpiece, wonderfully helpful and thought-provoking.

REFLECTION AND RESPONSE

We can never reflect too often on the Sermon on the Mount but now could be a time for particularly thinking of its application in our own lives and to respond where we see action is needed or a change of life required; and we should all keep praying for deeper love.

PART D

**GOD'S NEW COVENANT PEOPLE
BY THE TRIUMPH OF GRACE**

CHAPTER 13

God's strategic battle plan

Aim: To see the amazing strategy of God to open the minds of Jewish-thinking of Christians to accept Gentiles in the New Covenant on equal terms

FOCUS ON THE THEME:
The whole area had been blanketed with advertising that a new Tesco Store (with a shopping centre around it), was about to be opened. In a new area without any such facilities it was a welcome event. Crowds gathered. The Mayor gave a speech, praising Tesco's for their contribution to the neighbourhood and for a major gift to social needs in the borough. The tape was cut; the doors swung open; the crowds (including Myrtle and myself) surged forward. As we entered through the doors to the whole complex, an elderly couple asked one of the officials on duty: 'Which way is it to Sainsbury's?' They were not being funny. They had the fixed idea about Sainsbury's in their minds and all the advertising, speeches and neon signs over the Tesco entrance did not change their thinking. So it was with many Jews for some years after Pentecost. In spite of all of our Lord's teaching about the gospel to the world, they were still very deeply influenced by Jewish tradition. God had to change them.

Reading: Acts 9:1-19
Key verse: Acts 9:15

African dancers with music, drums, wonderful costumes and head-dresses, singing with Africans sounds, burst into the majestic setting of York Minster. It was St Andrew's Day 2005 and the occasion of John Sentamu, originally from Uganda, becoming Archbishop of York. The 3,500 people packed into the Minster were sharing in a magnificent service of solemnity and joy, and now there was this exciting feature too. It demonstrated the variety of the worldwide church, the inclusion of all peoples of any colour or ethnic background within the New Covenant family of Christ. Then, at the end of the service, the Minster became an even greater scene of colour as thousands of balloons were released. On these balloons was a message: 'Jesus said, follow me' and under those words was this: 'All are welcome'. Precisely right. The gospel of grace is open to all. The early church had to learn this.

The huge congregation, from every background, was then given an excellent picnic lunch. Some perched on any ledge or seat as they ate, others walked around, all were greeting one another – a real family atmosphere. The African singers and dancers cleared some of the chairs in the nave and went on celebrating. People joined in; the new Archbishop played the drums for a while. Yet everywhere you went, children, young people, women and men were walking around with the balloons attached to their hands declaring 'Jesus said, follow me . . . All are welcome'. The disciples could hardly have envisaged anything like it even in the excitement that followed Pentecost. The radical teaching of their Lord, the awakening to the meaning of the cross, the experience of the Holy Spirit, the proclaiming that Jesus was the Messiah, did not, at first, alter their Jewishness. Although they had heard our Lord say that they were to take the gospel to the whole world, the implications of this charge had not sunk in. A radical change needed to happen to the apostles. They needed to preach that all are welcome. God achieved it by going round them.

On the publications section of a computer there is a symbol that allows pictures to go behind or in front of other material. In God's campaign in Acts, he was bringing grace to the fore and moving law behind. The inclusiveness of grace was to be superimposed over the exclusiveness of law. God's strategy to bring about the change was, of course, brilliant. He first chose his key man for the task. Histories of conflicts through the ages show how important the commander is in any campaign. The battle would often be intense. It needed a leader of courageous conviction as his life would often be in danger. Nothing would enrage some Jews more than the idea of Gentiles being included as equals in the kingdom of God.

Only God would have chosen Saul of Tarsus. Only God could have seen the strengths, the learning, the wisdom and the one-track determination of the man and how he could bring all of those qualities to the spreading the gospel of salvation by grace. Only God could have brought about the man's conversion, and he did. Later on, in Philippians 3:12, Paul would write: 'I press on to take hold of that for which Christ Jesus took hold of me.' Whatever the conviction to his heart when he watched the wonderful way in which Stephen witnessed to Christ as he was being stoned to death (Acts 7:54-60); however much that convicting of his heart caused his terrible persecution of Christian men and women to begin, the experience on the Damascus road (Acts 9) was the most direct conversion challenge that anyone could have.

God blinds him temporarily; Jesus speaks to him; his response shows that he knows it is the Lord; he knows from the start that God has taken hold of him and he is under orders from the Lord: 'Now get up, and go into the city, and you will be told what you must do.' When Paul later appears before Agrippa, he says (Acts 26:16-18) that his call to the Gentiles was given there and then: 'I have appeared to you to appoint you as a servant and as a witness of what you have seen of me and what I will show you. I will rescue you from your own people and from the Gentiles. I am sending you to them to open their eyes and turn them from darkness to light, and from the power of Satan to God, so that they may receive forgiveness of sins and a place among those who are sanctified by faith in me.' By Acts 9:15 Ananias, afraid at first to go anywhere near Saul, is not only told to go and lay hands on Saul but also: 'This man is my chosen instrument to carry my name before the Gentiles'.

The new commander-to-be now grasps immediately that Jesus is the Messiah, the Son of God. He preaches this powerfully in the synagogues and the first conspiracy to kill him is hatched. God therefore takes him off (via the humbling experience of being lowered in a basket over the wall of the city in 9:25) We learn from his later letter to the Galatians (1:17) that he went off to Arabia for three years. I used to think that meant going off into the Sinai peninsula but then discovered that Arabia came up to the edges of Damascus. It would have been a local bus ride, if buses had existed then.

It was still desert and he presumably lived in the Bedouin manner. Here alone with God and with all his extensive understanding of the Old Testament Scriptures, Saul was taught and trained. He would emerge as God's trained commander in the battle for the message of salvation by grace alone to be spread to Jew and Gentile across the known world, a commander who was a brilliant theologian, with a brilliant mind and a courageous, pioneering, prayerful and strategically-thinking determination to uplift Jesus as the Messiah, the Saviour of the world.

So, with his commander ready and trained, what does the Lord do? He parks Saul back in Tarsus, for nine or ten years.

● *What did Saul feel, being parked? He must have been itching to get on with the job for which he was trained. He may well have had a number of local missions and these may account for some of the sufferings listed in 2 Corinthians 11 but he must have known he was not being used on God's major plan for the world.*

● *Now let's apply that to ourselves. Sometimes we may feel we are parked. We have all sorts of training for God's mission but perhaps are, at the moment, where we do not seem to be able to fulfil our calling. How should we act and respond? How stands our trust in our Lord? How is our patience? How is our serving where we are?*

● *If in a group, please discuss this. It will be made specific if any have experienced this or are experiencing it but the principles are worth working out regardless; it may prepare some for the future.*

As a boy, I loved to travel on the Atlantic Coast Express from London's Waterloo station. It was thrilling to look at the magnificent steam locomotive up front. What also fascinated me was that at several junction stations a section was detached and a small engine would take it off down a branch line to the sea eg at Lyme Regis or Sidmouth. They would be parked there until it was time to rejoin the Express. Then they would be brought out of their local station and put into position to rejoin the Express when it arrived. I loved it all, but especially the planning that had gone into it, with the set times for waiting and then rejoining. That is, in a way, what is happening in Acts. God's major Grace Express involves parking sections while others are sorted out and made ready to join the mainline journey. Eventually everything will be joined up and the journey will proceed with no delay.

Saul was parked because God had to deal with Peter. In Acts 9:31 Saul is parked in Tarsus; in 9:32 the cessation of persecution by Saul enables the church to settle and grow; in 9:32 we turn to Peter. A mere twelve verses later (10:1) we are into the next piece of God's strategy. Once again, we realise this is entirely the action of God. The Lord appears to a leading Gentile, Cornelius, and instructs him to send messengers to Peter's house in Joppa. They are already on their way when, at the right time for the link-up, Peter goes to his house-top to pray. He has the vision of the impure and unclean animals, with the Lord telling him nothing is impure that God has made clean. As he wonders what this means, Cornelius' three messengers arrive, exactly on God's timetable. The connection is made. Peter joins them and goes down the track to Cornelius' house in Caesarea. That he then goes inside a Gentile's house is a huge step for a Jew. He explains in 10:28 that he has done it because God had shown him that he should not call anyone unclean or impure. What followed when Peter preached the gospel, that Jesus is Lord of all: teaching, crucified, risen, Judge of all, that everyone who believes in him receives forgiveness of sins, was the second Pentecost. Later, Peter explains to the apostles (11:15) that the Holy Spirit fell on them as 'on us at the beginning.' He baptises them in the name of the Lord Jesus Christ (10:48). Peter is now ready for the mainline mission.

● *When any Christian has problems about the colour of someone else's skin or their ethnic background, they need to come back to this passage and repent. Two thousand years ago, Jesus changed Peter. Some churches I have been to have been entirely white and do not want or welcome*

*any other coloured skin. They sin against Christ if they are
in a mixed-race area. They are not on his mainline. Is there
any vestige of this in you (I ask myself the same)? Is there
any need for anyone in a group to go and put things right
with a sister or brother of a different skin colour?*

There was still someone else that God had to sort out before
the mainline mission could fully proceed. It was James,
head of the church in Jerusalem. It seems to me almost
certain that he was the Lord's brother. He had a passionate
and courageous sense of care for the poor and had an
enormous impact for Christ in Jerusalem but he was also
entrenched in his Jewish background and unlikely to be
much influenced otherwise in his Jerusalem surroundings.
He was happy for Gentiles to be converted but wanted
them to submit to Jewish customs. God begins the strategy
to change him a long distance away, in Antioch (Acts 11:19-
24). This was a strategic choice by the Lord. It was a huge
city of half a million inhabitants, the third most important in
the Roman Empire after Rome and Alexandria. It was a
very free and open city. Jews were open and liberal (in the
best sense of that word). The acceptance of Gentiles would
not have been a problem. It was here that converts from
Cyprus and Cyrene went and preached the gospel to
Greeks. When a large number believed, the news soon
spread to Jerusalem. The apostles needed to act. They
immediately chose Barnabas as the one to send. He was the
obvious choice. He had much earlier been the only one who
gave the right hand of fellowship to Saul in Jerusalem. He is
beautifully described as a good man and full of the Holy
Spirit. You can imagine him arriving with a smile on his
face and love in his heart. He encouraged them and the
mission grew as even more believed.

Barnabas realised this was the moment God wanted
Saul back on the mainline. James was still needing to be

joined up but Saul would be part of achieving that. So he goes and gets Saul from Tarsus. Saul and Barnabas had a great year in Antioch and it was during it that 'Christians' began to be used as a nickname. All was going well but later (Acts 15:1) the Judea party turned up in Antioch and starting preaching that Gentiles must be circumcised or else, they said, 'you cannot be saved.' It was pushing their view too far. Galatians 2:12 says that the James party caused Peter to draw back and even Barnabas. They were strongly opposed by Paul, and then by Barnabas and Paul. The issue now had to be sorted out. There needed to be a show-down in Jerusalem and so it happened. James had to chair the Council of Jerusalem and he eventually melted in the light of the testimony of Peter, Paul and Barnabas so that he could declare that they should not make things difficult for Gentile believers and only require not eating food offered to idols, avoiding sexual immorality and the meat of strangled animals and blood.

Now God has the whole 'train' joined up. He sets it down the line of his purposes. Once again there is direct intervention by God in Paul's life, as Paul finds the way blocked (Acts 16), the Holy Spirit preventing him going into the province of Asia, then the Spirit of Jesus preventing him from going into Bithynia, so that he ends up on the coast at Troas. God has got him where he has been planning to bring him from the beginning. Paul sees the vision of the man from Macedonia calling him to come over and help them. He sets sail and the gospel enters Europe at Philippi. It was an Aegean Express but eventually became the Atlantic coast Express and the Pacific Coast Express and the mission to the world. The strategy that began on the Damascus Road was now complete and the strategy to win Europe for Christ had begun. The limitations to the New Covenant gospel reaching the world had been overcome, even though there would many local battles ahead. The building of Christ's church could proceed throughout the world. It was a glorious moment in God's strategic plan for the New Covenant to be open to everyone everywhere.

● *Have you met or heard of Christians who insist that unless you do this, or have that experience, you will not be saved? How do you answer them? Why do you think they are like that?*

● *Are there any other traces of legalistic thinking or teaching that linger in your church, and in you? How much is grace obviously abounding?*

FURTHER STUDY

We have moved fairly swiftly across this history, so rereading it in the New Testament would be helpful: Acts 9:1 to 16:12.

REFLECTION AND RESPONSE

• I hope your spirit has been uplifted as we reflected on God's strategy to bring the Gentiles fully within his New Covenant people. Reflect on what may be God's strategy for advancing the gospel in the town or area where you live.

• Let us renew our commitment to doing what we still can to forward the mission of the gospel of Christ to the whole world, with a passion for those parts of the world where it is now almost too dangerous to be a Christian due to the religious hate and bigotry from others, but also for our neighbours and local area.

CHAPTER 14

Grace steadily triumphs

Aim: To see how grace was the basis of the covenant from the beginning and how, in the New Covenant, it liberates us and inspires us

FOCUS ON THE THEME:
Finding someone who could cater for large events at Bishop's House in Chester at a reasonable rate was frustrating, until someone suggested a farming lady who had gone into catering and who was an active Christian. Brenda readily agreed to help us and did so for all our events from then on, with wonderful meals, no fuss, a lot of joy, a great team and a very special price, as part of her Christian service. We were so grateful that, after some years, we asked her to come as our guest to London with her husband, and her co-leader and husband, to have a tour of the Houses of Parliament with lunch at the House of Lords. She leapt at the idea but her husband had never been to London and the whole idea of travelling there by train and coming to the House of Lords was definitely not in his orbit of thinking. Eventually he was persuaded to drop his barrier and he came. It was so lovely to see his utter joy, thrill and enthusiasm throughout the whole visit. We all had a wonderful time. That is what grace is like when the barriers of legalism are broken down. It is sheer joy and wonder as you discover all that you have missed out on for so long: not just for a day but for ever.

Readings: Ephesians 2:4-10; Galatians 2:15,16,19-21; Romans 4:25 – 5:5
Key verses: Ephesians 2:8; Romans 5:2

My heart almost burst with joy and thankfulness. At his Installation as the new Archbishop of York, John Sentamu uplifted Christ in his Sermon with heart-warming boldness and then declared to that huge congregation in the Minster, and those watching across the country by television, that his prayer on becoming Archbishop was 'that God will grant me an ever-increasing measure of discernment, so that, like the apostle Paul, I may fight for the truth of the gospel of salvation by grace alone.' It was glorious to hear. Salvation by grace alone – the heart of the gospel; the very fabric of being New Covenant people; the truth that liberates from legalism. Amen, Archbishop!

If ever someone knew what this meant, it was Paul. As a Pharisee he seems to have been one of the most legalistic of all and someone who fiercely defended that position and promoted it. In the powerful third chapter of Philippians, he sets out his pedigree as one who trusted 'in the flesh', i.e. in circumcision, who was of the special tribe of Benjamin, who was a Hebrew of Hebrews, of the law, a Pharisee; zealous in persecuting the church; faultless in righteousness based on the law. Not only was his conversion from that quite amazing but it was even more amazing that he saw immediately that Jesus was indeed the Messiah. He saw how the Messianic predictions in the Scriptures, on which he had been brought up, now made sense.

He also grasped at once that salvation was not in any way from the law but through faith in Christ. His passion was now for Christ, not for law. His message and mission are expressed with utter clarity in Ephesians 2:8, 'it is by grace that you have been saved, through faith – and this not from yourselves, it is the gift of God'. In more recent years Moffatt, the translator of the Scriptures, came to the firm conclusion that the religion of the Bible 'is a religion of grace or it is nothing . . . no grace, no gospel.'

As Paul walked down the gangplank at Neapolis, near Philippi, and his feet touched European soil for the first time, he must have wondered what lay ahead. As he walked the few miles to Philippi (Acts 16:12) he would no doubt have been praying about how to begin his mission there. In spite of his eagerness, he then waits on God for several days. He does not charge in but seeks God's strategy (good advice for evangelists). In that way he knows he will be likely to 'strike oil'. He had a fairly gentle induction as there were few Jews to oppose him in that dominantly Roman army city. He starts with the women (Jews and Jewish proselytes) meeting by the riverside (as there was probably no synagogue there at that time) and grace breaks through with Lydia, a Jewish proselyte, a wealthy merchant lady. The church in Philippi has begun.

However, although Jewish opposition was nil, the opposition from the commercial profiteers was strong. Paul was to discover that when grace touched and transformed the female servant who 'had a spirit' and her owners were going to lose their lucrative income from her, manipulation of authorities and whipping up the crowds in condemnation would be used (some newspapers do the same today). It would happen again later with the silversmiths in Ephesus (Acts 19:23-41).How well we know that today, with secularists and materialists using authorities, for instance, to ban the use of Christ in Christmas under the guise of it being politically correct to do so for the sake of other faiths. Yet the other faiths are not, on the whole, objecting. Secularists hate grace. So they find it bewildering, even embarrassing, when, as has happened recently in Liverpool, the Christian mother of a black boy, axed to death, forgives the racist attackers. Her amazing grace in forgiving was seen by most of the country on television and was stunning. That is grace triumphant. So it was in Philippi. In spite of the punishment and imprisonment wrought on Paul and his companions, even the jailor and his family believed and were baptised. Grace had triumphed over the attacks of secularism. The church grew.

● *Could we put ourselves in the position of that mother, with our lovely committed Christian son having been axed to death? Could we forgive? Is there anyone we have not forgiven and should now do so?*

In Thessalonica Paul goes straight for the Jews in their synagogue (Acts 17:1). He preaches the gospel and proves that Jesus is the Messiah. More time elapses than Acts 17 indicates, as a church seems to have begun in Jason's house. He and the other members must have been converted more than three days before the riot happened. All is fine, even while Paul is preaching Christ; even though there are Jewish converts. The violent reaction is triggered when 'God-fearing Greeks' (Acts 17:4) respond. The legalistic Jews cannot take this. The idea of Gentiles being included was beyond the pale for them. So there is a riot, a physical attack, the use of city officials, accusations of traitorship to Caesar, anything to stop grace breaking through to the Gentiles. Although Paul had to leave, grace triumphed wonderfully, as the letters to the Thessalonians show. Paul goes on to Berea where there is a great response and serious examining of the gospel message. Gentiles, Greek men and women, are converted. The Thessalonican Jews are enraged when the news of this reaches them and they go at once to Berea to stir up the crowds. They cannot bear the thought that Gentiles are being included.

The message of grace is bitterly opposed now by legalists (including legalists in the church who, for instance, regard the act of baptism or other sacraments and ceremonies as saving someone regardless of faith) and by secularists. One country church in the Diocese of Chester suffered from this. The fine Christian minister and his people needed to add a small extension to the building. It was a sensitive plan; the extension was almost completely hidden from view. The opposition in the village was fierce. On the grounds that it would spoil 'their' church (even if they did not go to it) the non-Christian villagers were whipped up. Every house was canvassed, the secularist authorities were invoked and everyone attended and overwhelmed parish church meetings. It was sickening. For that battle, the opposition won. But it has not stopped grace abounding in that village church since, any more than it was stopped in Philippi or Thessalonica or anywhere else. Grace can and does triumph, in the face of all the world's opposition, for it flows from the heart of our loving God and those who oppose it are opposing God.

● *Is there opposition to your faith by members of your family? Can you identify what causes it? Is it secularism, fear, ignorance, some warped picture of the church? Is it a legalistic form of Christianity? Grace in your life will convict them and may cause a sharp reaction, as it did for Paul. We have found young workers and students meeting violent reactions from their parents after they turn to Christ and start to live in a new way, by the grace of Christ.*

● *Pause to pray for those who are opposing your life as a committed Christian.*

● *Knowing the grace of the Lord in salvation is one thing but we need much daily grace from the Lord to live as a Christian in a hostile environment, be it in the home, at work, amongst friends, or especially in countries where opposition to Christianity is more or less required by religion. So prayer for much grace is essential.*

● *Are there those known to you who are under attack for their faith? Are you? Pause to pray for them and yourself to have more and more of God's limitless grace.*

Paul's letter to the Galatians is almost a manifesto to show how grace triumphs over law. Paul's heart aches. They are already deserting the one who called them by the grace of Christ. They are turning to another gospel, which is no gospel (1:6). He reminds them (2:11) how even Cephas (Peter) had wobbled under the pressure of messengers from James and had detached himself for a while from the Gentiles, how that affected others, even Barnabas. Paul had not been moved. He attacked and exposed the hypocrisy. Every sentence hits the mark: 'A person is not justified by observing the law, but by faith in Jesus Christ' (2:16).

Turning back to legalism would be to 'set aside the grace of God'(2:21) for anyone who has been 'crucified with Christ', and in whom Christ lives. He does not live by law any more but (v. 20) 'by faith in the Son of God, who loved me and gave himself for me.' We are children of grace.

Next, Paul brings in the Abraham argument. This is where it all began. Abraham (3:6) 'believed God, and it was credited to him as righteousness.' It was also to Abraham that the gospel was 'announced . . . in advance'. All nations would be blessed through him (3:8). The law introduced at Sinai had not altered this, for it was 430 years later (3:17). How did and do Jews overcome this clash? Some argue that Abraham lived a perfect life of 'natural law', that he lived the Ten Commandments without having received them and that he was therefore the original practiser of the law, keeping it in every detail. It is amazing to me that anyone swallows such an argument. Paul tears it to shreds in the rest of chapter 3, showing that law was introduced because of our sin and that it acts as a schoolmaster to lead us to Christ. Finally, in chapter 3, he gives us the great truth that we are all one in Christ Jesus, Jew, Gentile, slave, free, male, female and then, for his Jewish hearers he pushes it all back to Abraham with 'If you belong to Christ, then you are Abraham's seed, and heirs according to the promise' (3:29). Other arguments are included in Galatians and then there is an exultation in the freedom we have in Christ and life in the Spirit. No wonder he ends with 'The grace of our Lord Jesus Christ be with your spirit, brothers and sisters.'

● *I hope that was not too heavy but actually an exciting run through the doctrine that was so necessary then and still is today. Can you defend the faith and contend for it in terms of grace, in the face of legalistic religion?*

● *Within the Prayer Book service of 'Morning Prayer' and 'Evening Prayer' occur two special songs.* Benedictus *is the morning one. It is Zechariah's song from Luke 1:68-79. Please read it aloud. If in a group, please join in it together, or perhaps alternating verses between two halves of those present. Zechariah was singing at the birth of John the Baptiser and he knew that the coming birth of Jesus was a result of the Abraham Covenant (vv. 72,73).*

● *Turn to Mary's song (the* Magnificat*) in Luke 1:46-55. Again the connection is made (v. 55) to Abraham. The link to Abraham and the fulfilment of the covenant was grasped from the beginning and, in fact, Matthew begins with the genealogy of Jesus and the first name is Abraham. Moses is not included.*

● *One further mention of Abraham: In Luke 19 we have the much-loved story of Zacchaeus' dramatic conversion and of how Jesus says to him: 'Today salvation has come to this house, because this man, too, is a son of Abraham.'*

We cannot end this more doctrinal chapter without looking briefly at the exciting content of Romans 4. The whole chapter is headed in some versions 'Abraham Justified by Faith'. We are in the middle of the great evidence that all have sinned and fallen short of the glory of God, whether Jew or Gentile. We are about to have the gospel explained. But first Paul uses Abraham, to show that the gospel of Christ is the fulfilment of the Abraham Covenant of grace and faith. It is not something new. It is restoring what was meant from the beginning. It is going back to roots. The key phrase is here in verse 3, 'Abraham believed God, and it was credited to him as righteousness.' Then comes the next uppercut. It was credited to him before he was circumcised . . . *before*. So, although he was then circumcised as a sign of his faith and a seal of righteousness, he is father of those who believe though uncircumcised as well as of those who believe and are circumcised. Wham! It is a flattener of an argument. Paul then gives some final finishers as he points out that the covenant promise was not given through the law, and that Abraham was to be father of many nations, which meant far more than Jews. It is all (v. 16) by grace and is therefore guaranteed. And then comes the fruition of being right with God, and having access into his grace, which is amazing.

So it is our Christ-given responsibility to declare to all, whether in York Minster or a tiny village or the commercial centre of a city and everywhere in the world: 'By grace you are saved through faith in the Lord Jesus Christ.'

● *While writing this chapter I had a visit from a friend in ministry saying how so many church people in his country area seemed to have lost confidence in the gospel and its power to transform lives. I was appalled to hear it. What about you? I trust you have confidence in the gospel, zeal to share it and joy in living it, but if not, is it a moment to stop, pull your gospel self together and then go forward with fresh confidence and zeal? The gospel still is 'the power of God for the salvation of everyone who believes' (Rom. 1:16) whether we have confidence in it or not.*

FURTHER STUDY

We have covered so much Scripture in this chapter that the best study would be to go back slowly over it, reading much of Galatians, Ephesians 2, Romans 4 – 5.

REFLECTION AND RESPONSE

Meditate on what it means to you that you have been saved by grace through faith in the Lord Jesus Christ and then lift your heart in praise and thanks to your Saviour.

CHAPTER 15

You are family

Aim: To see how we are now the covenant family of God, through Christ

FOCUS ON THE THEME:
The recently-graduated Ghanaian was about to return home after his years of study in London. Could he say something in his final service at All Souls Langham Place? He said that when he first came to the church he kept hearing about 'the church family' and he tried to find out where this church family could be found or seen. 'Then,' he said, 'I realised that I could be part of this church family.' The whole concept had meant so much to him; he had experienced acceptance as a brother alongside other sisters and brothers from various nations of the world, all united in Christ. The church family was a family indeed and was also clearly part of the worldwide covenant family of God through Christ.

Reading: 1 Peter 2:4-10
Key verse: 1 Peter 2:9

Gentiles accepted by God on the same terms as Jews? We saw how that enraged strict Jews in Paul's ministry. Yet we need to empathise with their deeply-embedded belief that the Jewish nation was the family of God and all others could only be attached or associated. Attacking or altering that would be like knocking away the foundations beneath their feet. It is similar to the recent attitudes regarding males and females. The attitudes to women for centuries in Britain, regarding them somehow as second-class, unfit to vote, to be in the home bringing up the family and not in business, were challenged in the early part of the twentieth century but were largely smashed during the second world war, when women were needed to take over the jobs of men in the forces. Since then the skirmishes have continued, with fresh advances (or retreats, depending how you look at it) – a woman prime minister, women in business, women ordained to the church's ministry and so on. Even though the creation of humankind was male and female with no inequality signalled, the differences have persisted. The New Testament breaks down the separations between male and female; all are to be one in Christ. Yet males' sense of superiority persists even among Christians, 200 years on. In some non-Christian parts of the world (and even some Christian) male superiority is still appalling, untouched by Christ. Only recently a girl from such a country has been in the Miss World competition, braving fierce criticism, and has said how wonderful it is to be in a country (the UK) where women are equal to men.

That helps me to understand and feel the shock, the resistance, the anger felt by Jews who thought themselves superior to all other peoples, as God's chosen people, and were now being told that they were only God's chosen people by faith and that the Gentiles could be God's chosen people by the same means. John is unequivocal in his Gospel when he declares (1:12,13) 'Yet to all who received him, to those who believed in his name, he gave the right to become the children of God – children born not of natural descent, nor of human decision or a husband's will, but born of God.' Later we have the 'whoever believes in him' of John 3:16, and many other such references. The entrance to the covenant family (usually called the 'church' in the Epistles) is open to all who believe.

The clearest passage on our being God's covenant people is 1 Peter 2:9,10 which begins with the declaration: 'You are a chosen people'. This is a direct use of the Old Covenant term. It links us back to that lovely promise of Exodus 19:5: 'If you obey me fully and keep my covenant, then out of all nations you will be my treasured possession.' The term is used frequently and naturally through the Old Testament. For example:

> The people he chose for his inheritance (Ps. 33:12).

> My people, my chosen, the people I formed for myself (Is. 43:20,21).

> You only have I chosen of all the families of the earth (Amos 3:2).

It was deeply embedded in the psyche of the Jewish nation and suddenly it was adopted with transformed meaning in the coming of Christ and the New Covenant. The Old Covenant promises were transferring to the New.

It was a huge leap. Paul made it in one jump at his conversion. Peter took a little longer but by the time he writes this letter he takes it for granted. All the four phrases used here are Old Covenant phrases and Peter uses them of the New Covenant with ease. His grounds for using these phrases spring out of the earlier verses in the chapter where he goes back to the foundation stone, the 'chosen and precious cornerstone' foretold in Isaiah 28:16 and the promise there which Peter expresses as 'the one who trusts in him will never be put to shame.' Peter does not attack those holding on to the old but breathes the new; he does not even use the terms 'old' and 'new' but says 'you are a chosen people'; he does not refer to Israel as the chosen people but with refreshing openness sees all who believe on Christ, with no distinction between Jews and Gentiles, as God's chosen people. It is a declaration that would be breathtaking even today in some parts of the world.

Do you remember what it was like as a child to be chosen for some special task or responsibility or sports team? It felt good to be chosen. Put yourself in the position of an adopted child who knows she or he has been chosen. It is a comfortable feeling. Yet neither illustration is on target here. We are chosen people not because of talents of leadership or in sport; we are not chosen without a say in the matter as adopted children are as infants; we are called 'chosen' because we have believed on Christ, not for any merit or skill or works or achievement. It is not that only specially chosen people believe but that those who believe are then regarded as God's special family, his adopted children, his chosen ones.

● *So how much does it mean to us to nestle in the arms of our heavenly Father as one of his children, chosen and precious? Let us revel in the privilege and joy of this wonderful relationship, given by grace alone in response to faith.*

Although I was involved in the pioneering of new songs for Christian young people and in encouraging them to learn to play the guitar so that they could accompany them, I also increasingly had a longing to include in the leading of worship those who played orchestral instruments.

When I was able to appoint Noel Tredinnick as Director of Music at All Souls Langham Place in 1972, the starting of an orchestra became possible, thanks to his gifts and training. It has been the springboard for orchestral groups all over the country. I loved it and, as the years have gone on, with the great 'Prom Praise' events and others, I have increasingly appreciated the skills that are used to arrange music for orchestras and that can 'hear' how each instrument needs to be used. There is no room for individuality unless the conductor chooses and encourages it and only then do we hear splendid solo sections from the clarinet, the flute, the trumpet, the cello or whatever. Most of the time all the musicians are playing or pausing (some counting an enormous number of bars before their next part) so that the whole is effective. God's chosen people are a family but also, in a sense, an orchestra. We may enjoy being together, as an orchestra usually does, but like them we, corporately and individually, have a part to play.

So in 1 Peter 2:9 we are called a 'royal priesthood'. The Greek actually is 'king's priesthood' or a 'kingdom of priests' and that gives the role a direct responsibility to the King. This is a straight use of the Old Covenant description of the chosen people, as in Exodus 19:6, 'you will be for me a kingdom of priests'. So what did a priest do in the Old Covenant? He stood between the people and God, representing and acting for the people to God and declaring God's Word to the people. As we know, in the New Covenant, as set out in Hebrews, Jesus is the final priest and final High Priest for ever. We have (Heb. 10:19) 'confidence to enter the Most Holy Place by the blood of Jesus, by a new and living way opened for us through the curtain'. So we no longer need priests to be our go-between with God, because of Jesus.

How then can we be his priests? What is our role for him? We are to act in the name of Christ as his messengers to the world. He commissioned us to go into all the world to make disciples and in that sense we act as his priests in bringing the message of God in Christ to the world. On the other hand, we cannot represent people towards God except in prayer but we do have the responsibility of evangelism, of the personal endeavour to bring people across the faith-line into a living faith in Christ.

It is normal for ministers to urge congregational members to evangelise and witness but there is often hesitation on the part of the hearers. This is sometimes due to an uncertainty about how to do it. If I go into a street and there is someone bleeding to death from an accident, it is no use people screaming at me to do something as I am not trained in first aid. In evangelism we need training, help and practice. Learning from someone more experienced in the skill of witnessing was a help to me in early days.

● *So how able are you as a witness and evangelist? If you are in a group, why not split into twos and try it for five minutes, with one of you being the questioning atheist and the other the witness, perhaps about who Jesus is; then reverse roles and this time trying to explain the cross; and so on.*

I am not an extrovert and found it difficult to dive in from cold with evangelism, so I asked God, when a student on a vacation job in a hotel, whether I could promise to dive in whenever an opportunity opened itself. I thought I was safe in that hotel but then two days later the staff started talking about the Bible over tea and I dived in. It has been my rule, my 'method', ever since, except when wearing a clerical collar, as then I often have to dive in from cold and into the cold.

● *How about you? Talk it over with others. If in a group, share ways of witness you have been able to exercise fruitfully. You might like to adopt the pledge with God to open your mouth if he creates an opportunity.*

There is something more about our being a royal priesthood. In the Old Covenant the priests were worship leaders, playing the instruments and forming the choirs, as they declared in song and shouting 'His covenant love endures for ever'. So here in 1 Peter 2:9 it says 'that you may declare the praises of him who called you out of darkness into his wonderful light.' This is part of our responsibility as priests for our Lord; to be able to share our testimony of the way the Lord brought us to himself and to be able to explain just what it has meant to come out of darkness into his glorious light. Peter may have in mind the contrast for Gentiles of not being God's people and not having received mercy with becoming his people and recipients of his mercy. Others suggest he may even be anticipating the final glory when Christ comes to gather his family for ever.

Singing and praising are part of that, and it is glorious to share in it, but personal testimony is at the heart of the meaning. We see the power of such declaration in Acts with Peter's sermon and speeches, in Stephen's courageous witness and in Paul's testimony before authorities and in his writings.

Our testimony is firstly, of course, regarding how we came to faith. For some it will have been sudden, on a certain day and even at a particular time but for others, like me, it was more like the rising of the sun and the steady illuminating of my soul. I cannot give you a date. As Spurgeon is reported to have said, 'You do not have to know the date of your birthday to know you are alive!' Secondly, our testimony is about the light we have found in place of darkness, the way the Lord has opened our heart, changed our lives, our standards of living, our ambitions, our values and the whole purpose of living; the way we have joy and hope

● *A popular hymn says that this is 'my story' and 'my song'.*
  Can we think through what we have to testify about and how
  we might do so more effectively? Is it up to date and fresh?

Two other Old Covenant terms are used in 1 Peter 2:9,10 of
all of us in Christ. They are 'holy nation' and 'You are the
people belonging to God'. The first springs from the Old
Covenant promise of Exodus 19:6: 'You will be for me . . . a
holy nation' and the second especially from the New
Covenant prophecy of Jeremiah 31:33: 'I will be their God,
and they will be my people.' Peter uses them without any
reference to the past and as now clearly fulfilled in all
Christian believers.

He has already quoted in 1:15 'Be holy; because I am
holy' and this occurs several times in Leviticus, e.g. 19:2, to
lead into details on how to live as God's people. In our
next and final chapter we shall look at how Paul spells
this out for us. Yet there is also here a sense of God taking
his people through to the end against all the opposition of
the world and proving to the world that we are his people,
set apart by him and for him through Jesus our Saviour;
by grace triumphant.

FURTHER STUDY
Look in detail at the witnessing of Peter (Acts 2; 3; 4).

REFLECTION AND RESPONSE
• Reflect on 1 Peter 2 9,10 and revel in these glorious privileges
  given to you in Christ.

• Is action needed to be more truly what you are and are expected
  to be as a New Covenant person?

• Then reflect and give praise and thanks that you are 'God's
  special possession'.

CHAPTER 16

Living as God's covenant people

Aim: To learn from Paul of the range of differences in living that should be evident in covenant people

FOCUS ON THE THEME:
The Swiss mountain train climbed up and up towards the Jungfrau Mountains. It was the middle of the day and there was only a young American couple in the coach apart from Myrtle and myself. It was their first visit and they were so disappointed that the train was enshrouded in thick mist and visibility was almost nil. Then, suddenly, the train emerged above the mist into brilliant sunshine and there, right before their eyes, was the spectacular sight of the Jungfrau Mountain, the sun reflecting off the snow, the lower slopes in glorious green. Everything the eye could see was breathtakingly transformed with beauty. That couple will never forget the moment when they moved from darkness to light. We, who had seen it many times, were excited for them and with them. We could then show them where they were heading, way up at the top of the Jungfrau, where the final train would deliver them into the most amazing experience. They would soon be there.

Coming to Christ is the same. When the mist of spiritual blindness lifts, the light of Christ is overwhelming; even when it lifts slowly we gradually wake up to seeing him and what we see is increasingly thrilling. Yet we are also given

> the foretaste of the heaven to which we are heading and we
> know that then the experience will be amazing, as the
> whole covenant family of God in Christ is home together at
> last. We will be there, by grace triumphant.

*Readings: 2 Samuel 23:5 (the David Covenant); Colossians
3:1-17*
Key verses: Colossians 3:1-4; 3:12.

Loyalty to a football team or any other sports team seems
to overlook barriers. One of the July 2005 suicide bombers
in London was also a keen supporter of Manchester
United. The young British conductor who opened the
opera season at La Scala Opera House in December 2005
wore a Roy Keane (Manchester United) shirt in rehearsals.
Once the shirt is worn the barriers are temporarily down
and there is unity. Even in Myrtle and myself, there is still
a strong loyalty to the Manchester City football team
which began during our ministry in Manchester when the
parish was next to their ground. We left there in 1970 and
still 'support' even if we do not wear the shirt or attend
matches. City supporters are known for their fanatic
loyalty even when their team dropped divisions for a
while.

At first sight, it might seem that Christian oneness is
similar. We belong to Christ and have a loyalty to Christ.
In Ephesians 2:11-22 we have a passage that spells out this
unity. The Gentiles have been 'brought near through the
blood of Christ', the dividing wall of hostility has been
'destroyed' and the very titles of Jew and Gentile are
subsumed into 'one new humanity'. Now the comparison
with the football supporter becomes totally inadequate.
Away from the match (and sometimes sadly during the

match) the differences recur; the unity is temporary. In Christ the unity is permanent. It is to affect all of our lives. Everyone in Christ, says Ephesians 2, is reconciled through the cross, has peace with God, has access to the Father by the one Spirit. We are all fellow-citizens, one household, one building. That is all the result of the New Covenant and affects the whole of our thinking and living.

This could be a moment to cheer the powerful exposition Paul makes, except that we know that we as Christians can mar this purpose and can persist in disunity, even when we agree about Christ and the true gospel. Paul attacks disunity in 1 Corinthians. The Corinthians had fallen for the trap of dividing under different leaders but by the Second Letter it seems they had fallen even more seriously, by yielding to the influence of some very silver-tongued operators who were distracting them from the true gospel. Since then the church has known, and knows only too well today, separations under different labels of denominations or groupings or even under specific individuals with a charisma. We may all say we belong to Christ but sometimes we can allow secondary differences to assume a dividing importance; we can allow a personality to become a magnetic influence when loyalty is more to the person than the truth. Supporters can become seriously partisan. Paul throws down the gauntlet in 1 Corinthians 1:13: 'Is Christ divided?'

So, as New Covenant people, who have been made one in Christ and who are heading for one family in heaven, disunity here, other than over the non-negotiables of the gospel, is a disgrace to our Saviour and to what we are by grace. At the time of the ordination of women in the Church of England there were a few churches who broke fellowship with me as their Bishop. Members who had been warmly friends before would not even shake my hand; they would not share the same Communion Table. It grieved me very deeply because such a disagreement should never have broken oneness in Christ (indeed it could not do so). I would say to some of them 'If you and I died in the next five minutes, do you think our Lord would be concerned about whether we were for or against the ordination of women?'

Later in Ephesians 4:3,4, Paul urges us to 'Make every effort to keep the unity of the Spirit in the bonds of peace.' It does take effort, doesn't it? It takes effort to reach out to those of different age-groups, social background, denomination, affiliation and to those who worship in a different style to that which we prefer, but we must do so. It takes an effort for some Christians to rid themselves of a deep racism or sense of superiority over those of a different colour, but we must do so. Nelson Mandela said that after his release from imprisonment, when he began to travel widely, he found himself one day in a small plane in Kenya with a black pilot and momentarily he felt insecure, such was the depth of a sense of black inferiority imbued in him from birth. If he felt that after so many years of fighting apartheid it is not surprising if it requires a determined effort to eliminate such ideas from our minds, but we must do so. In Christ we are one family for ever and need to do all we can to make that a reality between Christians here and now.

- *Does this encourage your endeavours for unity in Christ? If so, is there more you can do, perhaps in helping others with more separatist attitudes?*
- *Or does it touch a nerve and stir the conscience? Will you take steps to sort this out, for Christ's sake?*
- *If in a group, you might like to think of differences known to you between Christians. Is there action you can take to bring about reconciliation between individuals or between members of different groupings?*

When I was eighteen, like all young men of that age in Britain, call-up papers arrived for National Service. Soon after, I travelled on the night train to Catterick Camp in Yorkshire to begin my Army service. After various preliminaries, cropping of hair, pledging of oaths, receiving of papers and allocation to a barrack room, we were marched to the uniform store to receive each item of uniform and other kit (no measuring, just thrust at you by guess-work). On return to the barrack room we were ordered to divest ourselves of civilian clothes and to put on our army uniform. Our 'civvies' had then to be packed into a brown paper parcel and sent home. We had completely 'put off' our civilian identity and had completely 'put on' our identity as a soldier. We were not allowed to wear civilian clothes during the first part of our training, and so were in uniform even during time off and going home on a weekend leave. We knew what it was to 'put off' and 'put on'.

In Ephesians 4:22-24 Paul urges us to act deliberately in a similar way: 'Put off your old self . . . put on the new self'. However, this is not ordered but urged on us. We have a choice not to do so. Although he does not use the term 'covenant people' it was basic to Paul that all his churches were New Covenant churches and so he uses several different terms: Christ's 'people' and 'the body of Christ' (4:12), 'dearly loved children' (5:1), 'God's holy people' (5:3). In Ephesians 4 and 5 he lists the things of darkness to be purged out of us such as falsehood, anger, stealing, unwholesome talk, bitterness, malice, greed, immorality; and he urges the new walking in the light of truth, honesty, forgiveness, kindness, helpful talk, sharing, compassion, understanding what the Lord's will is and so on. There can be dramatic action at conversion, like the man 'into' pornography who was converted one night at a major evangelistic rally and then went home, collected all his pornographic literature and threw it from the Albert Bridge into the Thames. That sort of outward action needs to happen where it can. However, much of the change is going to be within our thinking and our inner being and this needs us to 'be made new in the attitude of our minds', a process for life. I am sure you agree that we can easily fall into the comfort mode of comparing ourselves with some other Christians but Paul lifts our eyes in 4:24 saying the new self is 'created to be like God'. In 5:1 we are urged to follow God's example ('Be imitators of God') and in 5:10 we are to 'find out what pleases the Lord'. This includes the constant study of Scripture, always with a desire to hear, follow and respond; the discipline of meditation and chewing over what God is saying to us; the courage to act on what we know he is saying, is the way we change. There is no other way.

In Colossians 3:1-18, Paul is equally concerned but here he lifts our sights even higher. Now our resurrection status in Christ is picked up in verses 1-3. We are 'raised with Christ', our life is 'hidden with Christ in God.' Then our perspective is lifted to our eternal future: 'When Christ, who is your life, appears, then you also will appear with him in glory' (v. 4). We are preparing now for that eternal family and are to anticipate its purity, its unity, its love, and so on. 'Put off' becomes 'put to death' and 'put on' is followed by 'clothe yourselves' as 'God's chosen people' (i.e. New Covenant people). So we are to strip off the 'civvies' of our old selves and send them packing (and every time we realise there is something of the old remaining we are to do the same; we are to clothe ourselves (and keep re-clothing as we grow) with Christ's way in every aspect of our lives. Surely we should wear his 'uniform', his family clothing, with pride, not in ourselves but in him; be it at home, at school, at college, at work, at leisure or anywhere. Authorities in some places may ban the wearing of Christian symbols but they cannot stop us being clothed with Christ.

An asylum seeker, recently arrived in London, was walking past the church where we now worship. His attention was caught by its attractive notice board and he made a note of the telephone number. Later that day he telephoned for an appointment. When he came, he explained that he wanted to find out more about Christ and wanted to convert to Christianity. He had been working for an Aid organisation in his troubled home country and had been deeply struck by the love, integrity and hard-working commitment of the 'foreign' workers, all of whom were active Christians. He saw it as a sharp contrast to the standards of his fellow-countrymen. The lives of the Christians drew him to seek Christ for himself. Here in this London church he found him and came to a living faith in him. He was baptised. His hope has been to be allowed to stay here and study at a Bible College before returning home for Christ. He had not read a Bible before he came; he had read the lives of Christians, people clothed with Christ. It seems that today, in our own country, Christians are the only gospel that most people will read and so we have to show lives that are evidently different, not the same as others plus church on Sunday, but radically different, living in the clothing of Christ and with Christ as King.

- *I am feeling uncomfortable. What about you?*
- *I think of occasions when I have let Christ down and although I have sought forgiveness, the shame still stings;*
- *I wonder how often I might have put people off Christ;*
- *I start another review in my mind of how we live and according to what values;*
- *I ask the Lord to help me to go on putting off and putting on;*

● *I tell him how I long to please him every day.*
● *What about you?*

Now we are not just on the final segment of our covenant journey but we are looking forward to the great family reunion, for ever. We missed out one of the main covenants earlier because it seemed right to include it now. Much is rightly made of the Davidic Covenant because it speaks of the eternal nature of the covenant. In 2 Samuel 23:5 David speaks of God having made with him 'an everlasting covenant' but earlier in 2 Samuel 7:13,14 the promise is messianic when God says of a future successor in David's line: 'I will establish the throne of his kingdom for ever. I will be his father, and he shall be my son.'

Isaiah 55:3 then addresses all who are thirsty and who come to the Lord for his rich provision and to hear what he says, with these words: 'I will make an everlasting covenant with you, my faithful love promised to David.' It is this love that holds us now and through into eternity. It is the same rich covenant language when Paul exclaims in Romans 8:38: 'I am convinced that neither death nor life, neither angels nor demons, neither the present nor the future, nor any powers, neither height nor depth, nor anything else in all creation, will be able to separate us from the love of God that is in Christ Jesus our Lord.' What security. What assurance.

It is a glorious comfort to all of us mortals that, in Christ, our very being is eternal. It is a privilege to have ministered at the bedside of many Christians in their last days or hours. Quite often I have read the end of 2 Corinthians 4 and the start of chapter 5, with the rich descriptions of what is unseen being eternal, the glory ahead that far outweighs all our present troubles, that we will be clothed with our heavenly dwelling so that 'what is mortal may be swallowed up by life' and then, finally, in

5:8, 'We are confident, I say, and would prefer to be away from the body and at home with the Lord.' At home with the Lord – the culmination of our earthly membership of his covenant family. Several times, I have felt myself on holy ground as the Lord Jesus comes to take a dear saint to himself; some speak of music; some have a face relaxing into a gentle smile; all have his peace and, after prayer, I have often felt I must go quietly from the room as they slip into the welcoming presence of their Saviour, home at last.

● *Have you been present at such a moment with a believing relative or friend? Reflect on John 14:1-3 and be assured.*
● *If in a group, do share your experiences.*

The fresh breeze of eternity keeps sweeping into the New Testament and gives anticipation to our souls. With Abraham, where God's covenant promise by grace, through faith, began, we are 'looking forward to the city with foundations, whose architect and builder is God' (Heb. 11.10); we know that we are 'citizens of heaven' and that Christ will 'transform our lowly bodies so that they will be like his glorious body' (Phil. 3:20,21); we are thrilled at the prospect of the trumpet call of God, of his family being gathered and that 'we will be with the Lord for ever' (1 Thes. 4:16,17); we anticipate with impatient excitement the 'new heavens and a new earth in which righteousness dwells' (2 Pet. 3:13, NKJV). Yes, these passages are accompanied with the challenges such as 'What kind of person ought you to be?' so that we more truly live as the future family right now, but, at this moment, just allow yourself to be gathered up with the anticipation of glory.

Come in your mind and stand in heaven. See yourself joining in the song of praise to the Creator in Revelation 4 and let your eyes notice the rainbow (v. 3), the covenant sign with Noah. Feel gathered up in the vast throng of Revelation 5 as you see 10,000 times 10,000 angels and the vast throng caught up in praise and adoration: 'Worthy is the Lamb, who was slain, to receive power and wealth and wisdom and strength and honour and glory and praise' and then, as part of the redeemed, covenant-loved family of God, we shall cry 'Amen!' This is the end and the beginning; this is the culmination of God's covenant love; this is God's covenant people home together at last; this is the triumph of grace.

FURTHER STUDY

Search out the many other passages in Paul's letters and 1 John that describe how we should live as God's holy people; or look in more detail at the sections of Ephesians and Colossians we have quoted above.

REFLECTION AND RESPONSE

- You may like to go on reflecting what this last section of the chapter means to you. Do you have the same assurance? If so, give thanks and enjoy thinking about it with your Lord.

- Are you uncertain, perhaps finding it a bit embarrassing? Do seek help from someone else who knows their Bible and has assurance or keep rereading the passages used in this chapter.

- Finally, why not quietly or corporately say or sing the hymn Amazing Grace?

AMAZING GRACE

John Newton's much-loved hymn sums up the theme of Grace Triumphant and could be an appropriate vehicle for your own response.

1. Amazing grace – how sweet the sound –
   that saved a wretch like me!
   I once was lost, but now am found;
   was blind, but now I see.

2. God's grace first taught my heart to fear,
   his grace my fears relieved;
   how precious did that grace appear
   the hour I first believed!

3 Through every danger, trial and snare
   I have already come;
   his grace has brought me safe thus far,
   and grace will lead me home.

4 The Lord has promised good to me
   his word my hope secures;
   my shield and stronghold he shall be
   as long as life endures.

5. And when this earthly life is past,
and mortal cares shall cease,
I shall possess with Christ at last
eternal joy and peace.

John Newton (1725–1807)

END NOTES

[1] Sheldon Vanauken, *A Severe Mercy* (London: Hodder and Stoughton, 1977)

[2] Bishop James Jones, *Jesus and the Earth* (London: SPCK, 2003)

[3] Russell Stannard, *God for the 21st Century* (London: SPCK, 2000)

[4] Charles R. Swindoll, *Moses* (Nashville: Word Publishing, 1999)

[5] Edward W. Goodrick and John R. Kohlenberger, NIV *Exhaustive Concordance* (Grand Rapids: Zondervan, 1990)

[6] John W. Stott, *Christ the Controversialist* (Leicester: IVP, 1996)

Keswick Ministries was set up in response to demand to take the excellent Bible teaching of the three week summertime Lake District Keswick Convention and make it available throughout the year and around the world. Its work is aimed at Christians of all backgrounds who have a desire to learn from God's Word and let it change their lives.

Keswick Ministries is committed to achieving its aims by:

- providing Bible based training courses for church leaders, youth workers and young people, preachers and teachers and all those who want to develop their skills and learn more

- promoting the use of books, tapes, videos and CDs so that Keswick's teaching ministry is brought to a wider audience at home and abroad

- producing TV and radio programmes so that superb Bible talks can be broadcast to you at home

- publishing up to date details of Keswick's exciting news and events on our website so that you can access material and purchase Keswick products on-line

- publicising Bible teaching events in the UK and overseas so that Christians of all ages are encouraged to attend 'Keswick' meetings closer to home and grow in their faith

- putting the residential accommodation of the Convention Centre at the disposal of churches, youth groups, Christian organisations and many others, at very reasonable rates, for holidays and outdoor activities in a stunning location

If you'd like more details please look at our website (www.keswickministries.org) or contact the General Director by post, email or telephone as given below.

Keswick Ministries, PO Box 6, Keswick, Cumbria, CA12 4GJ
Tel: 017687 80075
Fax 017687 75276
Email: centre@keswickconv.com